Santa Maria
Country Club
and
Its History

By

Ollie M. Kirby

Janaway Publishing
Santa Maria, California
2017

Published by

Janaway Publishing, Inc.
732 Kelsey Ct.
Santa Maria, California 93454
(805) 925-1038
www.JanawayPublishing.com

2017

ISBN: 978-1-59641-386-3

Cover photograph of *The Lone Golfer*
by
Robert Rande Downer

Made in the United States of America

This book is dedicated to ALL the people who have been a part of this wonderful piece of heaven right here on earth, known as the SANTA MARIA COUNTRY CLUB.

Thanks not only to the people who created it, but also thanks to all the terrific people who have cared for it and maintained it for the past 95 years.

COVER STORY

————•◆•————

The front cover of this book portrays the awesome beauty of the 18th fairway. The photographer, Rande Downer, spent numerous hours and days waiting for just the right lighting and shadows to capture this image. And he waited for just the right subject to come strolling down the fairway approaching the 18th green. He entitled the photograph, *Lone Golfer.*

The back cover shows three pictures as follows:

1. The original building. This was cropped from a very long picture which hangs in the clubhouse office. When and by whom it was taken is unknown. The author took it, frame and all, down to Arrow Camera in town and requested they NOT take it out of the frame. They managed to shoot the image down through the glass, since the old material is very fragile. Note the beautiful old historic cars.
2. The second building picture was provided by Dick Weldon. When and by whom it was taken is unknown. Where he had to take it to get it "cleaned up" is for him to tell. I am grateful to Dick for his kindness.
3. The modern new clubhouse picture was provided by Bert Mayor, longtime employee in the office at the clubhouse. She also is editor for the monthly newsletter, *The Sandbagger.* She is also the person who influenced me the most in undertaking the writing of this book.

CONTENTS

————•◆•————

Part 3: Santa Maria Country Club Staff

PREFACE

———•◆•———

This is a history book, but it is so much more. The author introduces you to not only the beginning era of the Santa Maria Country Club, but to more recent persons and events which are shaping its new history. An article, "Origins of Golf," is also included for readers who, like the author, have a limited knowledge of the game of golf.

This book attempts to bring to life not only the "shakers and movers" involved in the formation of the Santa Maria Country Club, but the "roll-up-your-sleeves" working folks. The first chapter begins with an article, believed to have been written by the late Maurice Twitchell, entitled *Origins of Golf.*

As substantiated by legal documents provided to me by Dick Weldon, the first formation meeting of what was to become the Santa Maria Country Club, was held in the Directors Room of the Bank of Santa Maria at 2:00 P.M. on November 21, 1921. At that first meeting, the seven (7) participants each purchased one share of stock for $100.00. Those seven participants were:

L. C. Palmtag, Frank J. McCoy, George M. Scott, F. J. Goble, J. H. Chambers, N. B. Libbey, and M. Thorner.

All seven were elected to serve on the board of directors. Frank J. McCoy was elected President, and N. B. Libbey was appointed as temporary Secretary.

Golf, at the beginning era, was a man's pastime played primarily by the wealthy. But the everyday working men also had big dreams. They toiled away at their jobs and wanted "play time" too. Ranchers, farmers, oil-field workers, merchants and others came together to develop a golf course in Santa Maria. For a $100.00 share of stock they could be a part of the dream; in fact, it was from the ranks of these folks that many shares were sold.

It was three years, and quite a few headaches later, before the 9-hole, 160-acre site was ready for play.

Then the Great Depression hit with a vengeance. Some of the shareholders couldn't pay their monthly assessment of $7.50. The club lowered the monthly assessment to $5.50 per month and they still couldn't pay it, and they lost their shares. The bank loan went into default and the club was on the verge of foreclosure. The sale of 80 acres of SMCC land to Mr. Waller of the Waller-Franklin Seed Company for $6,500 cured the default and the club survived.

Times began to improve in the 1940s. World War II brought an influx of military personnel both at Hancock Field and Camp Cooke. Also, the discovery of oil in Orcutt contributed to the economy of the area. The Santa Maria Country Club signed a lease with Union Oil, and two producing wells were drilled on SMCC land.

In 1946, the Ladies Division was organized. They had six lady golfers. Jayne Evans was their first President. Ladies Day was Wednesday.

After oil was discovered on SMCC property, a dispute arose between members. Those who had suffered through the Great Depression felt that new members should not be entitled to any of the oil royalties. The end result was that two separate types of memberships were established, and the Santa Maria Country Club filed papers on January 6, 1947 for incorporation as a nonprofit.

Construction of the back nine began in 1951. After the Santa Maria Country Club became a beautiful 18-hole course in the 1950s, it attracted many great players such as Sam Sneed, Bing Crosby, Tony Penna, Tommy Bolt, George Bayer, Lloyd Mangram, Eric Monte, Paul Runion and Lawrence Welk.

The California State Open was played at Santa Maria Country Club seventeen different years between 1957 and 1979. SMCC member Jack O'Keefe won the Open here in 1963.

After the clubhouse caught fire in 1954, it was rebuilt, remodeled and expanded. They added locker rooms, dining room, and a bar in the southeast corner. A swimming pool was added, and a pro shop. Tennis courts were not built until 1977.

The population of Santa Maria increased from 39,685 in 1980 to 77,423 in 2000 when the new clubhouse and all of its facilities (except the tennis courts) were completely rebuilt. The author's writings are about people, their lives, and events prior to 2000. It is up to some new author to document 2000 forward history.

ACKNOWLEDGMENTS

———•◆•———

There are so many people who should be recognized, and they are all local Santa Marians, so I will only mention a top few, without whose help, this book could not have been written.

1. My husband, Eldon Kirby. Living with a writer isn't easy. Maybe now he will get a "home cooked" meal more often!
2. Bert Mayor, who made me aware that a book had never been written permanently documenting Santa Maria Country Club history.
3. Tony Cossa. He had documented a lot of "bare bones" facts for slide presentations to civic organizations such as the Rotary Club. Tony is a 4th generation Santa Marian. He shared all the information he had put together on SMCC. He also introduced me to Rande Downer and showed me Rande's wonderful photography that graces the cover of this book.
4. Dick Weldon, Attorney. He was born and raised in Santa Maria, and his love for this city knows no bounds. I had never met him until I walked into his office and requested an interview. He loves history, especially Santa Maria history. And he has an incredible memory which amazes everyone I've talked with who has had dealings with him.
5. Sally Scaroni. At 99 years young and legally blind, she has not lost one bit of her keen intellect. All of the very old pictures and material on the Women's Division were provided by Sally. I try not to tax her strength, as she tires easily. I enjoy reading to her as she was always an avid reader before she lost her sight, and she enjoys keeping up with what is going on.
6. Rande Downer. I can't thank him enough for all the photography he did.
7. Susan Brown Evans. I didn't have a good photo of her father, Stan Brown, but she did. She also provided me with aerial photos taken by her mother, Vinnie Lee Brown, of the Sinton-Brown Feedlots.
8. Milton Guggia Sr., Vickie Guggia, Traci Guggia, and Rosemarie Vanetti Bullock. They all worked very hard to provide me with the history of the Peter Guggia family dating back to 1901.
9. Jane Drenon and Sandy Adams for their assistance and support during this

enormous undertaking. They were always there for me, providing encouragement.

I would like to express my heartfelt thanks to ALL of those who have taken time to share with me their experience and history with the Santa Maria Country Club. It was a joy meeting with every one of you.

PART 1

CLUB HISTORY
AND
ACTIVITIES

ORIGINS OF GOLF

———•◆•———

It is well known that golf originated in Scotland, probably at St. Andrews, about 1450. The original Scottish courses were built on links land. Links land consists mainly of sand deposited on the Scottish seashores by the action of ocean storms. Links land is similar to the Pismo Beach – Oceano sand dunes and the sandy areas along the ocean at Vandenberg Air Force Base.

Much of the links land in Scotland was common land and publicly owned. The four courses at St. Andrews to this day are all city owned and constructed on public land. Many courses in Scotland are still owned by the public, and the public has access to the links land through the designated paths through the courses.

The early Scottish links land courses were laid out and routed through natural valleys between the low sand mounds and hills. These valleys were sheltered from the winds where natural grasses grew. Turf grasses were later introduced. Very little land was excavated or moved. Therefore, to a large extent, nature designed the early Scottish courses and man only utilized the natural routes.

In the 1800s, it was discovered that the hearth land in the London area of southern England was also suitable for golf courses. A number of courses were built in southern England. These courses became known as "parkland courses" since they were not located on links land.

The MacDonald boys playing golf, by 18th-century portrait painter Jeremiah Davison.

While there were golf courses in the United States during the colonial period, golf did not become popular until after the Civil War, particularly in the 1880s and 1890s. A number of courses were built in the eastern United States.

As golf became more popular in England and in the United States, a demand for golf course designers arose. Initially, in England and Scotland most courses were designed by golfers, usually professional golfers. Many of the early Scottish links courses were redesigned by the expert golfers of the day.

When golf began to develop in the United States, Scottish and English players were imported to design the courses. There was a surge in the popularity of golf in the years before World War I.

In the years after World War I, through the 1920s, golf became extremely popular in the United States. There was a trend for designing and building golf courses for the "masses". The early courses in the late 1800s were built primarily for the wealthy.

Many of the courses built for the masses before and after World War I were built in the same manner as the early links courses, utilizing natural contours with very little excavation or earth movement. Mechanized earth movers, such as bulldozers and mechanized scrapers, were not developed until the 1930s. All shaping of the land prior to the 1930s had to be done with Fresno scrapers powered by teams of horses or mules, and by hand labor. Therefore, unless substantial financial resources were available, courses were designed and built with the idea of utilizing natural terrain as much as possible.

The design of these early courses for the masses also was crude and rudimentary. Sometimes courses were designed, laid out and staked in only a few hours. The designer would inspect the land and then stake the location for tees and greens. The members or developers would thereafter build the tees and greens in the designated locations. The designer would have no part in the actual construction of the golf course.

NOTE: All of the above was excerpted from material developed and compiled by Maurice Twitchell and Dick Weldon.

EARLY HISTORY OF THE SANTA MARIA COUNTRY CLUB

———•◆•———

On November 16, 1921 the first organizational meeting was held in the Directors Room of the Bank of Santa Maria. This meeting kicked off a chain of events. A few weeks later the initial acquisition for the front side property was negotiated. This land at the time included what is now our front side and all of what today is Waller Park. The purchase price of $9,000.00 was financed by offering shares of $100.00 each. Ninety-two Santa Marians took advantage of this opportunity, and the initial ground work for the Santa Maria Country Club was underway.

The first Board of Directors was formed in 1922, headed by President Frank J. McCoy (owner of the Santa Maria Inn), Vice-President George M. Scott, Secretary-Treasurer N. B. Libbey, and the following Directors: L. C. Palmtag, J. H. Chambers, Fred J. Goble, and Dr. M.

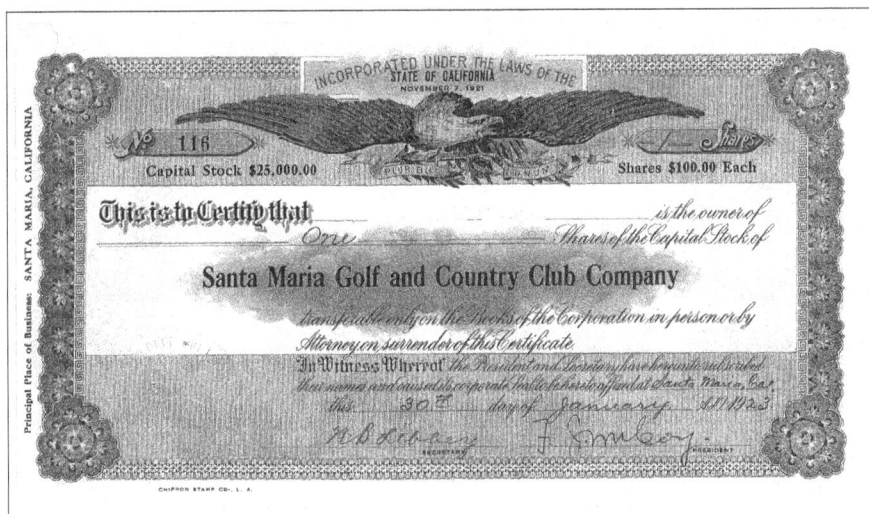

Stock Certificate issued by Santa Maria Country Club.

Thorner. In this same year, the Directors voted to build a club house at a cost of $2,860.00. The membership was assessed monthly dues of $7.50 which was reduced to $5.50 during the depression years that followed.

During this period, a watering system was installed. Materials for this project were donated to the Club by the Union Sugar and Union Oil Companies.

Financial difficulties struck the Club in 1927, and to alleviate the burdens of the time, eighty acres of the original property was sold to Mr. Waller of the Waller-Franklin Seed Company for $6,500.00. Mr. Waller later donated the property to Santa Barbara County for use as a park. It was initially named Washington Grove but was later renamed Waller Park.

Director George Scott, Opening Day at SMCC in 1921.

Following the depression years and progressing on to more prosperous times, in the fall of 1935 a young vacationing golf professional visited Santa Maria. His name was Frank Hocknell. Twelve years later he returned and became our Club's Golf Professional. Frank, along with others, was instrumental in molding our club and course into an improved configuration.

**Frank Hocknell, SMCC Golf Pro,
1947-1977**

Until 1946 the Club was limited to a nine-hole course but it was obvious that increased local growth, a rising membership, and an increasing interest in the game itself, would necessitate further future development. It was at this time that what today is our back nine was acquired on a long-term lease arrangement from the county.

In 1947, the Santa Maria Country Club assumed the position of a non-profit corporation. It had originally been set up in 1921 as a for-profit company known as Santa Maria Golf and Country Club Company.

Directors for the new non-profit corporation were: T. A. Twitchell, Dr. A. M. Beekler, K. E. Trefts, W. B. Johnson, Alec Stracken, Marion B. Rice, and C. L. Kyle.

With Ken Trefts as president in 1951, construction and development of the back nine began. With a group of dedicated and hard-working individuals, and with the generous support of local produce farmers who donated tractors and equipment, development of the back section was underway.

The forming and design of this awesome project was under the supervision and direction of Kris Kortner, Superintendent of Greens, from the inception of the course until his retirement, and also our dedicated Golf Professional Frank Hocknell.

The first major tragedy occurred May 31, 1954 when a fire gutted the clubhouse, leaving things in a temporary shambles. However, enough of the original building was left intact, and along with what was salvaged, the clean-up and reconstruction was soon underway. The cause of the fire was unknown. There are a few gaps in the history, and a few trophies were burned. During this timeframe a swimming pool was added, and in 1964 a new pro shop was constructed.

On May 31, 1954, a major fire gutted the SMCC clubhouse.

In 1965 the Club had a stroke of good luck when Don Buckley joined the pro shop. Don and his family came from Texas (originally from Nebraska) and the U.S. Army, from which he retired after over 20 years to his country. Don worked his five-year apprenticeship under Frank Hocknell's watchful eye, and in 1969 received his Class A card following graduation from P.G.A. school.

1973 was a major highlight year. The complete course belonged to the membership. This goal was reached following nearly two years of negotiations with the Airport Board for the purchase of the originally leased-back side of the SMCC property. The purchase price of $160,000.00 was available from the balance remaining from the sale of memberships in 1971.

Ten golfers at SMCC, ca. 1950s. L to R: Paul Cook, Charlie Cossa, Ken Trefts, Cap Twitchell, Blake Cauvet, Hal Twyford, Bink Rubel, Al Melville, Dr. Al Beekler, and Frank Hocknell.

The 1960 California Elks Championship Golf Team. L to R: Dick Weldon, Leo Steinberg, Coach Frank Hocknell, D. Paul Sanchez, Jack O'Keefe, and Stan Brown.

Pro-President, Riveria Country Club, 1959. L to R: Unknown, Unknown, Ken Trefts, and Frank Hocknell.

Lester Hayes, driving in the late 40s.

Cap Twitchell putting out on 18th hole. (Note the oil derrick in background.)

Cap Twitchell (left) and Ken Trefts (right).

Minutes of

First Meeting of Organizers and Subscribers to Stock of

Santa Maria Golf and Country Club Company

Held at the Directors Room of The Bank of Santa Maria in the Bank of Santa Maria Building, Santa Maria California on the 16th day of November 19.2.1, at the hour of two

o'clock P. M., pursuant to the following written consent and waiver of notice, to wit:

We, the undersigned, being all of the organizers and subscribers to stock of the

Santa Maria Golf and Country Club Company,

hereby give our written consent to the holding of the first meeting of the organizers

and subscribers to stock of said Company, at in the Directors Room of The Bank of Santa Maria, in the Bank of Santa Maria Building, Santa Maria, California , on the 16th day of November, 1921,

at the hour of 2:00 o'clock P... M., for the purpose of accepting and ratify-

ing the Articles of Incorporation filed by the organizers, ratifying the appointment

of the Directors named therein, and adopting By-Laws; and we hereby waive fur-

ther notice of the time and place of such meeting.

Dated at Santa Maria, Cal the 16th November, 1921

Name	No. Shares Subscribed for
L. C. Palentay	1 Share
F. J. McCoy	1 Share
J. M. Lewis	1 share
F. J. Goble	1 share
J. H. Chambers	1 share
N. B. Libbey	1 Share
M. Horne	1 Share

FIRST MEETING OF DIRECTORS
November 16, 1921

3

FIRST MEETING OF DIRECTORS
OF THE

Santa Maria Golf and Country Club Company

Held at the Directors Room of The Bank of Santa Maria in the Bank of Santa Maria Building, Santa Maria, California on the 16th day of November 19 21, at the hour of 2:00 o'clock P. M., pursuant to the following written consent and waiver of notice:

We, the undersigned, being all of the Directors of *Santa Maria Golf and Country Club* Company, hereby give our written consent to the holding of a meeting of the Board of Directors of said Company, at in the Directors Room of The Bank of Santa Maria in the Bank of Santa Maria Building Santa Maria, Calif on the 16th day of November 19 21, at the hour of 2:30 o'clock, P. M., for the purpose of organizing the Board, electing officers, and transacting such other business as may properly come before the Board; and we hereby waive further notice of the time and place of such meeting.

Dated at *Santa Maria*, the 16th day of *November*, 19 21.

L. E. Palmtag

F J McCoy

F J Goble

J W Chambers

N. B. Libbey

M Thomer

Present: L C Palmtag, F J McCoy, G M Scott, F J Goble, J W Chambers, N B Libbey M Thomer

CERTIFICATE OF INCORPORATION
STATE OF CALIFORNIA
SECRETARY OF STATE
June 14, 1951

State of California

Office of the
Secretary of State

I, FRANK M. JORDAN, *Secretary of State of the State of California, hereby certify:*

That I have compared the annexed transcript with the RECORD *on file in my office, of which it purports to be a copy, and that the same is a full, true and correct copy thereof.*

IN WITNESS WHEREOF, *I hereunto set my hand and affix the Great Seal of the State of California, at Sacramento, this* 14 th day of June, 1951

Secretary of State

By _____
Deputy

1   ARTICLES OF INCORPORATION

2   FOR

3   SANTA MARIA COUNTRY CLUB, a non-profit corporation.

4 KNOW ALL MEN BY THESE PRESENTS:

5   That we, the undersigned, T. A. TWITCHELL, A. M. BEEKLER,

6 K. E. TREFTS, W. B. JOHNSON, ALEC STRACHEN, MARION B. RICE and

7 C. L. KYLE, do hereby associate ourselves as the first directors

8 for the purpose of forming a corporation under Title XII, Article 1

9 of the "General Non-profit Corporation Law" of the State of

10 California and in conformity with such law, make the following

11 resolution and statement:

12   I

13   The name of the corporation is Santa Maria Country Club,

14 a non-profit organization.

15   II

16   The purpose for which the corporation is formed is:

17   a. The association is a club to be organized and operated

18 exclusively for social, pleasure, recreation and other non-profit-

19 able purposes, no part of the net earnings of which shall inure

20 to the benefit of any member. Among the general purposes is to

21 provide golf and other recreation to the members and guests of

22 such corporation.

23   b. To lease, purchase, hold and use and take possession

24 of and enjoy in fee simple or otherwise any personal or real

25 property necessary for the uses and purposes of the corporation

26 and to sell, lease, deed in trust, mortgage, pledge, alien or

27 dispose of the same at the pleasure of the corporation and for the

28 uses and purposes for which said corporation is formed; to buy

29 and sell real or personal property and to apply the proceeds of

30 sale, including any and all income, to the uses and purposes of the

31 corporation.

32

E N D O R S E D
F I L E D
in the office of the Secretary of State
of the State of California

JAN 6 - 1947

FRANK M. JORDAN, Secretary of State
By CHARLES F. GOING
Deputy

- 1 -

TWITCHELL AND RICE
ATTORNEYS AT LAW
SANTA MARIA, CALIFORNIA

III

The corporation is one which does not contemplate pecuniary gain or profit to the members thereof.

IV

That the existence of this corporation is to be perpetual.

V

That the County in the State of California where the principal office for the transaction of the business of this corporation is to be located is Santa Barbara County.

VI

That the number of directors shall be seven and that the names and addresses of the persons who are to act in the capacity of directors until the selection of their successors and the titles to be given to such directors are as follows:

W. B. Johnson (President), 115 West Hermosa Street, Santa Maria, California.

Marion B. Rice (Vice-President), East Camino Collegio, Santa Maria, California.

T. A. Twitchell, 157 Palm Court, Santa Maria, California.

A. M. Beekler, 301 East Chapel Street, Santa Maria, California.

K. E. Trefts, 164 Palm Court, Santa Maria, California.

Alec Strachen, 524 East Cypress Street, Santa Maria, California.

C. L. Kyle, 625 East Orange Street, Santa Maria, California.

The number of persons named above shall constitute the number of directors of this corporation until changed by the by-laws or an amendment to the by-laws increasing or decreasing the number of directors as may be desired.

VII

The authorized number and qualifications of members of this corporation, the different classes of membership, the property, voting, and other rights and privileges of each class

- 2 -

16

1 of membership, and the liability of each or all classes to dues or
2 assessments, and the method of collection thereof shall be as
3 is set forth in the by-laws of this corporation.

4   VIII

5   The name under which the hereinafter signed individuals
6 are associating themselves and the name under which such associa-
7 tion is being incorporated is "Santa Maria Country Club, a non-
8 profit corporation."

9   IN WITNESS WHEREOF, we have hereunto set our hands this
10 *18th* day of December, 1946.

11
12   W. B. Johnson
                            Incorporator and first director
13   Marion B. Rice
                            Incorporator and first director
14
15   T. A. Twitchell
                            Incorporator and first director
16   A. M. Beekler
                            Incorporator and first director
17
18   K. E. Trefts
                            Incorporator and first director
19   Alex Strachen
                            Incorporator and first director
20
21   C. L. Kyle
                            Incorporator and first director
22
23
24
25
26
27
28
29
30
31
32

- 3 -

THE STORY OF THE SPHINXES

———— • ◆ • ————

SPHINX USED IN THE FILMING OF CECIL DE MILLE'S "THE TEN COMMANDMENTS".

ENTRANCE TO SANTA MARIA GOLF COURSE, SANTA MARIA, CALIFORNIA.

To appreciate the significance of the postcard showing the two sphinxes at the entrance to the Santa Maria Country Club, you first need to know about the filming of *The Ten Commandments* in the Guadalupe dunes.

The year was 1923. Modern technology for the filming had not even come into existence yet. Cecil B. DeMille needed to film *The Ten Commandments* on site where there was a vast area of sand dunes. Traveling overseas with a large cast and crew to film was out of the question.

Frank McCoy, and others, evidently influenced DeMille's decision to film near Guadalupe where there were ample sand dunes to film. Guadalupe had one stipulation — after filming, the dunes had to be restored to their natural condition.

With a cast and crew of over 2,000 people to house, they built a "tent city." Getting supplies to the site was another consideration. They built the "tent city" and it was quite a boom to the local economy.

Paramount Studios had authorized Cecil B. DeMille a budget of $750,000 for the film. Weather delays and other problems arose. DeMille needed more money. When costs were approaching $700,000, Paramount telegraphed DeMille to stop production and return to Los Angeles. Instead, he took out a personal loan and waived his guaranteed percentage of the gross from the film. A.P. Gianinni's bank came to the rescue. DeMille went right on filming and completed *The Ten Commandments.* One article shows that the final budget was $1,475,837 and the box office proceeds were $4,160,790. The film was a big success. What DeMille wound up with after paying off his debts is unknown, but the film's success firmly established him as a director.

Sally Scaroni recalls that her husband, Paul, told her that his father, Leo Scaroni, took him out to the filming site when he was about 6 years old. He wasn't impressed with the place, but getting to go with his father was a treat.

When filming of *The Ten Commandments* was completed and the site had to be restored to its natural state, DeMille's crew buried the property underneath the sand. Pieces had been fabricated in Los Angeles and transported to the dunes where they were assembled on site.

The two sphinxes on the postcard escaped being buried under the sand dunes. How, and by whom, they were moved to the entrance of the Santa Maria Country Club, is still a mystery and will probably remain so. Smuggling them to that location would not have been an easy feat. They each weighed 5 tons! One thing is evident. They wouldn't have lasted too long as they were probably made of plaster of Paris.

Peter Scaroni (grandson of Leo Scaroni) loaned me a book entitled *Biography of a Bank,* the story of Bank of America N.T. & S.A. In Chapter 12, *The Santa Maria Episode and Its Consequences,* it talks about how A. P. Gianinni (Bank of Italy at that time) had attempted to get a branch bank established in Santa Maria back in 1923.

Peter Scaroni also gave me an old photo from a newspaper clipping which was among his grandfather's things when he died. The interesting thing about the photo (taken in Santa Maria circa 1936) is that all three people in the photo were Bank of America employees.

Santa Maria, CA circa 1936. Leo P. Scaroni, A.P. Gianini, & Lawrence Lavagnino Sr. Picture courtesy of Peter Scaroni, grandson of Leo P. Scaroni.

SPHINX #3 — DeGasparis SPHINX

When Tony Cossa gave me the old postcard photo of the two sphinxes guarding the entrance to the Santa Maria Country Club, I presumed they were the ONLY ones that escaped being buried underneath the Guadalupe Dunes after the filming of *The Ten Commandments.*

When I showed Dick Weldon what I had written he said, "You might want to talk to Ernie DeGasparis. I think his family has a very old photo of his ancestors seated on one of the sphinxes out in Guadalupe."

Ernie put me in touch with his sister, Mary "DeeDee" (DeGasperas) Green and her husband, Steve. They provided me with a copy of a very old photo showing four of their ancestors seated on a sphinx. There were also five other people, names unknown, perched on the sphinx.

Rumors abound concerning other sphinxes that escaped being buried. One rumor is that two of them wound up at the entrance to the Morganti Ranch. There is no way of knowing if this is true or not.

Man at bottom right is Ernesto DeGasparis (Ernie's grandfather), above him to left is, Attilio DeGasparis (Ernie's Father), above him to right is Catherine DeGasparis (Ernie's grandmother), and under the chin of the sphinx is Lucy DeGasparis (Ernie's aunt).

KRIS KORTNER

———•◆•———

The author had the privilege of talking by phone on July 13, 2016 with the son of Kris Kortner, SMCC Greens Keeper, from 1924 to 1970. His name is also Kris. He lives in Southern California, but had just been back to Santa Maria to attend his 70th Class Reunion at Santa Maria High School. Dick Weldon was also in that class and Kris had given Dick his phone number.

Kris has fond memories of growing up in Santa Maria when it was a small town. Many of the old landmarks have disappeared. He drove out to the Santa Maria Country Club and looked at the new facility. He remembered well the old 9-hole golf course where his father was the greens keeper from the time of its inception until he retired in 1970. He learned to play golf there. He went away to college in Southern California after graduation from Santa Maria High.

Kris is now retired and no longer plays golf. He never married so there is no future Kris Kortner in his family tree. He had two sisters who are both deceased.

Kris Kortner - Greens Keeper 1924-1970

THE INCREDIBLE STORY OF KEN TREFTS
(1902 – 1991)

———•◆•———

When my husband purchased Loal Huffman's membership in the Santa Maria Country Club, the Ken Trefts Member-Guest Tournament came up as a topic of conversation. I asked, "Who was Ken Trefts?"

I was in for a unique and wonderful history lesson. Ken was born on a dairy farm in Newman, California in 1902. He became an auditor for Union Oil Company, working out of their plant in Newman, CA. His audit territory included Santa Maria.

Participants in the Ken Trefts Member-Guest Tournament, 1972.
L to R: Ken Trefts, Unknown, Jess Vallely, and Charlie Cossa.

In 1930, he was offered the Texaco Distributorship in Santa Maria, and in the mid-1930s he joined the Santa Maria Country Club. He served on the Board of Directors from 1943-1963.

His leadership qualities had become evident early on. He gained the respect and trust of the large number of local agricultural members of the club. He was the most influential and longest presiding member the club ever had.

In 1951, under Trefts' leadership, construction of an additional 9 holes took place. Ken organized members for an all-out work party. They donated use of their tractors, graders, plows and other necessary equipment, plus their labor, and actually built the course!

Ken Trefts' involvement in the community was much in evidence as well. He served on the Santa Maria City Council (1940-1944). He was Past Exalted Ruler of the Santa Maria Elks Lodge 1538 from 1938 to 1939.

Ken served as the Santa Maria Country Club's President from 1947-1960. He later became an honorary member of SMCC until his death in 1991.

In 1966, when the SMCC Member-Guest Tournament was started, Ken Trefts was the logical person to be honored for his many long years of service to the Santa Maria Country Club.

SMCC FIRST GOLF CARTS

———•◆•———

The first golf carts at the Santa Maria Country Club (pictured above) came into existence in the 1940s. They were built in Santa Maria by a local craftsman. They were 3-wheel-gas powered Cushman scooters with a bench seat across the front, seating three players, and the driver seated behind. The golf clubs had to ride up front with the players.

There doesn't seem to be any record of who the occupants are in the above photo. The carts evidently weren't in existence for very long before they were replaced by more modern carts.

OIL

———•◆•———

After meeting with Jon Iverson, Associate Oil & Gas Engineer, State of California, Department of Conservation, Division of Oil, Gas, & Geothermal Resources in Orcutt on June 16, 2016, the history of the two oil wells that were located on the Santa Maria Country Club is as follows:

Well #1: Sunray Oil Corporation out of Tulsa, Oklahoma, began drilling on October 20, 1946, and completed drilling on November 8, 1946. They drilled to a depth of 5,588 feet where they found good quality crude. On October 14, 1971, they filed papers for abandonment of the well and pulled out.

Well #2: Sunray Oil Corporation out of Tulsa, Oklahoma, began drilling on February 28, 1947. They drilled to a depth of 5,536 feet where they found good quality crude. On March 13, 1984, they filed papers for abandonment of the well and pulled out.

Apparently then everything was transferred back to Union Oil Company, which assumed liability from thereon.

There is no way of assessing the impact of oil on the Santa Maria Country Club. When "Old Maude" ushered in the "black gold rush" in 1904, and the "people rush" began in Orcutt, which was 17 years before the Santa Maria Country Club came into being. Oil wells had sprouted up all over the Santa Maria Valley, and I mean ALL OVER.

The Great Depression hit Santa Maria hard. Some of the initial shareholders lost their shares because they couldn't pay their assessments. The Country Club was in danger of foreclosure for nonpayment of debt. The only thing that kept that from happening was the sale in 1927 of 40 acres of the original property to Mr. Waller of the Waller-Franklin Seed Company for $6,500, which was sufficient to satisfy the debt. Those 40 acres are now Waller Park.

In 1921, when the Santa Maria Country Club was incorporated as a "for profit" club, the population of Santa Maria was about 4,000. The only history notes show that 92 Santa Marians took advantage of the opportunity to buy $100 shares. Sally Scaroni says her father-in-law, Leo Scaroni, bought 5 shares at $100 each.

After surviving the Great Depression and the additional hardships of World War II, things were looking up. Union Oil Company and the Santa Maria Country Club entered into a lease agreement which resulted in two oil wells being drilled on the SMCC property. The picture below shows the location of the two wells. The steel oil derrick barely visible on the right of the middle row of trees is Well #1. The location of Well #2 is left of Well #1. It is unknown who shot this photo, but the photographer's timing was fantastic! The wells were located between #2 green and the #17 Tee box and to the right of #3 green.

The discovery of oil on the Santa Maria Country Club property brought about some "discussions" about who should receive income from the oil. In 1921, SMCC had been incorporated as a "for profit" corporation. The initial shareholders, who had suffered through all the hard times, felt that it was unfair for the influx of new members to share in the income from the oil lease.

The final result was the filing of new incorporation documents as a "non-profit" corporation. For some time there were two different classes of membership. Today, "equity" members own the club and are governed through a Board of Directors.

During the time the oil lease was in effect Sally Scaroni says she received an annual check for $25.00 for her one share of stock.

THE AIRPORT CONNECTION

———•◆•———

The connection between the airport and the Santa Maria Country Club didn't come about until 1946 when the need for more land to build an additional nine holes on the course arose. The additional land needed was acquired on a long-term lease arrangement with the county.

In 1973, following nearly two years of negotiations with the Airport Board, the leased portion of the west side of the railroad tracks was purchased, and the entire course was owned by the Santa Maria Country Club.

What is now the Santa Maria Airport, was built by the U. S. Army during World War II, and was known as Santa Maria Army Air Field. Its initial mission was to provide training for B-25 bomber pilots. That flight training was abandoned by December 1942. Then in September 1943, the arrival of the Lockheed P-38 twin-engine fighter plane gave the Santa Maria Army Airfield new life.

Lieutenant Wayne Warner

After World War II, Santa Barbara County and the City of Santa Maria, acquired the land and its facilities through two grants in 1948. Santa Maria Army Airfield was renamed Santa Maria Public Airport.

Public airport terminal – passenger services at left. Wayne Warner's crop duster fleet in foreground – early 1950s.

Wayne E. Warner was born October 8, 1918 in WaKeeney, Kansas. He became an Army Air Corps pilot and served in World War II. Included herein are three very old pictures of him in his Army Air Corps uniforms.

**Wayne Warner,
Army Air Corps Pilot**

After Wayne got out of the Army, he bought several World War II surplus Stearman airplanes and modified them for crop dusting, operating out of the Santa Maria Airport. Included herein is a picture which was included in Jim May's book, *Fifty Fabulous Years,* which shows Wayne's crop dusting fleet parked alongside the old Santa Maria Airport building.

Wayne and his wife, Mildred, joined the Santa Maria Country Club around 1956. By this time they had two daughters, Kara and Linda. Wayne didn't golf, but both Mildred and daughter Linda did. Included in the chapter on the Women's Division there are pictures of both mother and daughter.

Wayne started giving flying lessons to his older daughter, Kara. When she turned sixteen and got her driver's license her focus was on "her own wheels" and getting a car! I imagine "boys" also came into her focus.

After Wayne's death, a longtime friend saw his death notice in the Santa Maria Times and wrote a letter to the Editor. The print on the article is so old I took the liberty of typing it so it is legible:

Remembering the exploits of a longtime airport hero

To the Editor:

I am writing this story after seeing the notice of the passing of a longtime friend of mine from the early days of the Santa Maria Public Airport, Wayne Warner.

Wayne will always be a hero type to several other people besides me and they and I sure owe him their lives.

One early morning Wayne and his helper were loading his Stearman crop duster when a light plane carrying four people landed to take on some fuel, as I had not yet arrived for work yet they decided to go on. When I did get to work and opened the big hanger doors there in front of them stood a four place plane with the left wheel laying beneath it. On the door hung a note instructing me to get the parts to put it back in flying condition and the owner would contact me later. It was signed by a Captain in the California National Guard. He and three others were on their way to maneuvers in San Luis Obispo.

As they took off Wayne and his helper saw the left wheel fall off, the helper ran after the wheel and handed it up to Wayne in the cockpit. Wayne took off in his heavy loaded duster, chased after the other plane, getting near enough to hold up the wheel with both hands while flying with the stick between his knees and making sure the other pilot understood his problem, they both came back here. The pilot of the light plane was also a very skillful flier as all the damage to his plane was in the landing gear assembly.

Had it not been for Wayne and his skill as a pilot four good men could have been killed that day.

P.S. Wayne used to come into Millie's restaurant to get coffee and breakfast smelling like a chemical plant, after he flew in the mornings. Millie's was in the hanger."

George A. Doul A&E

SM PS 1948/1952

Lt. Warner, center, back row

THE RANCHO MARIA CONNECTION

———•◆•———

When Casa De Golf, Inc., who owned Rancho Maria Golf Club, was about to lose the golf course in 1970, four members of the Santa Maria Country Club formed a partnership and bought the ailing course. The four partners were:

John P. "Jack" O'Keefe, President
Keith Adams, Vice-President
H. Stanley Brown, Vice-President
James T. "Jim" O'Keefe, Secretary-Treasurer

The two O'Keefe brothers assumed the active partner roles in Rancho Maria, while Keith Adams and Stan Brown remained with Santa Maria Country Club. Another SMCC member who went to Rancho Maria Golf Club was Carroll Sharp, who had served as assistant golf pro at SMCC under Frank Hocknell. The move was a step up to head pro at Rancho Maria.

Jack O'Keefe had won the State Open at Santa Maria Country Club in 1963 (the same year that Rancho Maria had been constructed by Architect Al Boldock.)

Rancho Maria is a public golf course which has done well. It is still owned by the above-listed owners or their heirs.

THE WOMEN'S DIVISION

———•◆•———

In 1946, Ken Trefts and Bill Johnson invited Jayne Evans to the Men's Board Meeting of the Santa Maria Country Club. The men asked Jayne if she would organize the women to help "fix up" the clubhouse, which was one large room with a fireplace and the bare necessities in the kitchen.

The men were hoping to make SMCC more of a country club and attract more members. All of the men worked during the week, so the few women (about 6 regular women golfers) pretty much had the nine-hole golf course to themselves.

The women took a sewing machine to the clubhouse and made curtains. They held rummage sales and enchilada sales to raise money to buy furniture. Then the members enjoyed a catered dinner at the refurbished clubhouse, but most thought the meal was too expensive. So after that, it was potluck and BYOB. Below is a picture of the Santa Maria BBQ Team which was a large group, in 1949.

Santa Maria Country Club BBQ March 1949

Jayne Evans served as President of the Women's Division for the first two years. Ladies day was Wednesday. Each player paid a quarter before teeing off, and at the end of the day's play, the money was divided among the winners. Later, when the fee was raised from 25 cents to 50 cents, one irate member quit! All members played nine holes, came into the clubhouse, ate their sack lunches together, and then those who had the time (and desire) often would play cards or play another nine holes of golf. One needs to remember, the course at that time was not the manicured course you see today. When you were in the rough, FORGET IT!

Women's Board, 1953-54. L to R: Maurine Twyford, Tournament Chair; Delia Holmes, Telephone; Norma Twyford, Bridge; Jean Hoey, Treasurer; Sally Scaroni, President; Martha Lincoln, Publicity; Phyllis McCusker, Secretary.

The first evidence that any minutes were taken was in 1949 when Mary Hughes was the third President of the Women's Division. No by-laws had been written. In 1953, Sally Scaroni organized a committee to write the by-laws. By that time, the Women's Division averaged 15 players a week.

Included herein are copies of old Kodak camera shots taken in 1954, by Sally Scaroni, showing the long skirts lady golfers wore at that time. She was glad to see those become HISTORY.

The 1953-54 photo of the Women's Board was taken on the East side of the clubhouse before the 1954 fire which destroyed some of the history records and some of the trophies.

By 1979, hemlines had gone up and for a couple of years club members even bought cute matching attire. Too bad the photo can't be in color as the photo shows green and white.

Kentucky Fried Chicken sponsored quite a few tournaments at the Santa Maria Country Club, both men's and women's, in the 1970s. Sally Scaroni won in the KFC tournament in 1971 when she beat out Helen Mahan, Women's Division President, in a play-off.

Charlie Vest, Santa Marian, who was responsible for getting KFC to sponsor many tournaments at SMCC.

Sally Scaroni (right) accepting the KFC Trophy from Helen Mahan.

WAYNE AND MILDRED WARNER

The story of this couple is somewhat different since his life and death are covered in the story about the *Airport Connection.* Her story is all about golf.

They joined the Santa Maria Country Club around 1956. Mildred was an avid golfer. During her 38 years with the Women's Division, she won many trophies and awards. Playing golf at the Santa Maria Country Club was one of the great joys of Mildred's life. Another was teaching her grandson, Kris Dutra, to play golf at the Santa Maria Country Club.

Wayne and Mildred had two daughters, Kara and Linda. Kara wasn't interested in golf but Linda loved the game. In 1960, Mildred and Linda were winners in the mother/daughter tournament. In October of that same year, Linda won a trophy in the girls program.

Mildred continued to play golf at SMCC until 1996 when health issues forced her to give up the game.

Mildred Warner

Salinas Golf and Country Club
THIRD LADIES INVITATIONAL
MAY 25 and 26, 1967

Country Club Champs

These boys and girls proved to be the class of the field Wednesday at the Santa Maria Country Club Junior Club championship tournaments. John Knudsen won the boys division and Ann Harrington the girls division. From left to right in the front row are: Linda Warner, Vicki Harsin, and Miss Harrington. In the back row: Ray Varcoe, John Knudsen, Carl Cicero and Carl Engle.

Mother-Daughter Winners

These women and girls were the winners in the annual Mother-Daughters golf tournament held at the Santa Maria Country Club Tuesday. Leona Gile was the proxy mother for Vicky Harsin. They won the first flight with a combined total of 74. Linda and Mildred Warner took the second flight with their 48. From left to right: Leona Gile, Vicky Harsin, Linda Warner and Mildred Warner. Runners-up in the first flight were Flo Littlejohn and Toni Wiley. Pat Hilman and Terry Brownell placed second in the second flight. A. Diani sponsored the tourney. —Times Photo.

16 LADIES
"B" TEAM

Photo courtesy of Jane Drenon
Identification courtesy of Evelyn Portman

Front Row L to R: Rosemary Doud, Jane Drenon, Angie Crisafi, Irene Reynolds
Middle Row L to R: Emily Kreins, Evelyn Portman, Glenda Natzke, June Shimizu, Tonja Thurston, Diane Walburn. Barbara Diyorio
Back Row: L to R: Norma Hull, Helen Draper, Barbara Eggert, Betty Malone, Dottie Lyons

STEVE CUTTS AND HIS GIRLS
2011 "B" TEAM CLINIC

L to R: Jane Drenon (she didn't let the fact that she had just undergone chemo and lost all her hair keep her off the golf course!); Linda Ryan (she had a good time and didn't get too "up tight" even if her game wasn't going super.); Judy Green (a very talented and fun-loving lady); Steve Cutts; June Shimizu (a serious-minded golfer — Steve brought out a rare smile); Sandi Johnson (what a friendly, happy bundle of talent); and Sharon Sparrow (works hard to improve her game).

WOMEN'S GOLFING APPAREL IN 1954

Below are photographs taken by Sally Scaroni in 1954, showing the golf attire worn by lady golfers at that time.

Valera Gray, Hilda Hartmen,
Unknown, Phyllis McCusker

Unknown, Erma Wahrmund,
Virgina Guggia, Kay Hancock

Delia Holmes, Evie Ure

Inez Geoffroy, Adela Becktler,
Ida Toma, Virginia Guggia, Martha Lincoln

Dorothy Winter Bissen, Marge Branter,
Kathy Scaroni Brown, Phyllis McCusker,
Virginia Guggia

Ida Toma, Inez Geoffroy, Irene Cossa,
Adela Becktler

43

WOMEN'S GOLFING APPAREL IN 1979

By 1979, hemlines had gone up and for a couple of years club members even bought cute matching attire. Too bad the photo can't be in color as the photos shows green and white.

Carol Norwood, Pat Apple

Pam Fairey, Alice Huffman

Wilma Hesselbarth, Lori Sandona, Martha Vanetti

Wilma Hesselbarth, Marie Wineman

Fran Baxter, Jinx Kirk

Sally Scaroni, Myrna Pollock

GOLFING GRANDMOTHERS

What is known today as "Golfing Grandmothers & Others" originated in 1957 as a social club within the Women's Division of SMCC. It was conceived by two proud grandmothers, Martha Lincoln and Marion Hardy. It was a relaxed group, initially called "Grandmothers Club", who would meet, play golf, have lunch, and then some of them would stay and play cards. No by-laws were ever written up.

It caught on so well that many grandmothers joined into this relaxed group and it became apparent that they needed to organize the club in some fashion to establish accountability for various functions.

Early history records for the club are almost nonexistent. The first organizational notes that were hand-written and retained were in 1991. They show: President, Marge Santens; Tournament Chair, Phyllis Green; Secretary, Fran Cuneo; Treasurer, June Jackson; Publicity, Merle Sutherlin.

At some point in time, "Duties of Officers" were written, and each incoming officer received a copy at the beginning of the year. Also, somewhere along the way, Grandmothers Club transitioned to Golfing Grandmothers then Golfing Grandmothers and Others."

Following low attendance and participation, at the end of 2015, the structure of Golfing Grandmothers and Others was abolished, the bank account was closed, and the group decided to become a "Pay as You Play" group.

Martha Lincoln

TENNIS

————•◆•————

The origins of the game of tennis can be traced to a 12th-13th-century French handball game called *jen de paume* (game of the palm.) The word "tennis" evolved from the monks, who would shout the word *tenez,* the French word for "to take" while they served the ball.

Tennis did not become popular in the United States until the late 1800s. In 1874, the first tennis courts appeared in the United States.

The first Wimbledon tennis tournament (England) was held in 1877. During that first year, it only consisted of men's singles; women were not allowed to play until 1884. Players were clad in hats and ties!

Tennis is now not only one of the most widely played sports in the world, but among the most lucrative. And Wimbledon is the pinnacle for which players strive.

TENNIS AT THE SANTA MARIA COUNTRY CLUB

Tennis got off to a slow start at the Santa Maria Country Club. That is easy to understand, since SMCC started out as a "Santa Maria Golf and Country Club." Tennis players had to go elsewhere to play tennis. That all changed in the late 1970s. At the request of some of the other tennis players, Betty Couey got an audience with the Board of Directors to talk about getting tennis courts built and having a tennis club.

At that time, Bob Cooper was President of the Board of Directors (1974-1979.) There were many well-known members of SMCC who played tennis as well as golf. There were many factors to be considered, so the board asked her to come back in a month and they would let her know what they had decided. When she returned the following month, the board said there were several stipulations to them granting approval of the building of the tennis courts. The first was money. The tennis group had to sell 100 tennis memberships at $100 each. No "pledges" or promises. The next stipulation was that the Tennis Club had to be self-sustaining. And they had to come up with a Tennis Pro.

Selling 100 tennis memberships was no small feat, but lots of people responded. Then they got Gary Messick to be their first Tennis Professional. Work finally began. Some golfers complained about the fact that they lost part of their practice range to make way for the tennis courts. A few of the lady golfers complained about the tennis girls being allowed in the clubhouse in their cute tennis attire (didn't hear of any MEN complaining!)

The tennis courts were finally completed and opened in 1977. Betty Couey was chosen as the first Tennis Committee President who acted as a "go between" with the SMCC. That position continued, with numerous Presidents, until a major change occurred in the Tennis Club.

Photo courtesy of Betty Couey

Doctor's Tournament 1979 (sponsored by all doctors who were members)
L to R: Vickie Ramirez Simas, Shawn Gill, Dr. Dave Carty, Betty Couey, Kristy Becker.

1979 Doctor's Tournament:
L to R: Ned Johnson, Gene Robinson, Dave Carty, Dave Hollerbach, Jim
Cusack, Betty Tibbs, Bill Tibles. (all were doctors)

October 1979 Contractor's Tournament:
L to R: Corkey Wood, Pat Wood, Eileen Wood (contractor sponsor), Betty Couey, Mike Polley.

CIACA Women's Doubles Tournament
L to R: Betty Couey, Maria Van Hammerstein, Melva Kennison (sponsor), Vickie (Ramirez) Simas;
Jeri Ferini.

"A" Division 1st Place Maria and Herb Von Hammerstein 2nd Place Betty Couey and Mike Polley.

"B" Division 1st Place Carol Robinson and Bill Couey
2nd Place Noreen Prandini and Jim Iwasko.

May 1978 Calcutta - Bill Watkins and Betty Couey Won "A" Division

Photo courtesy of Betty Couey

Sister Act: Missy, Kacie and Krista Guggia
1994 Joined Tennis Club

Darien Wright, 1994

CENTRAL COAST TENNIS
AT
SANTA MARIA COUNTRY CLUB

Keith Bowker and Darien Wright have operated the Tennis Club since 1998.

A major change took place in tennis at the Santa Maria Country Club in the 1990s. Darien Wright began working on February 6, 1995, as Assistant Program Director in charge of Junior Player Development.

Born in Ladybrand, South Africa, Darien began playing tennis at the age of 12 under the coaching of her father, Keith Bowker.

In 1989-90 she won the Florida state championships for junior colleges singles and doubles. She graduated from the University of Florida (Gainesville) with a BS in Sports Science.

Upon arriving in California, Darien became the Assistant Coach for the Cal Poly University Women's Team In 1993 and completed her Masters in Exercise Physiology from Cal Poly in May 1994. She also taught tennis at Foxenwood Tennis and Swim Club, and she was the Assistant Coach for Righetti Varsity Girls Tennis Team during the 1994 season. Her husband, Graham, is also from South Africa.

1998 — THE DAWN OF A NEW AREA FOR TENNIS AT SMCC.

Keith Bowker and Darien Wright formed a partnership and were hired by SMCC in 1998, on a contract basis, to operate the tennis club. The following information was provided by them.

There were approximately 88 family memberships. If you had a golf membership, you could add tennis for a small fee. At that time, tennis memberships were family memberships. Tennis membership numbers grew really fast and were capped out at 155 family memberships.

We introduced junior tennis memberships to allow junior players, whose parents did not play tennis, an opportunity to play.

We purchased the Santa Maria Open tournament from the city and brought it to the Santa Maria Country Club. It is now one of the premier Open level tournaments in California, and brings both local and international players into Santa Maria for three days each year over the Labor Day weekend.

We introduced a junior version of the Santa Maria Open, the *Santa Maria Junior Grand Prix,* and this annual tournament attracts between 120-150 junior tennis players from all over the United States.

When we took over the management of the tennis program, there was only one ladies team in the Central Coast Women's Tennis League (CCWTL). Now there are three or four teams competing in the league on an annual basis.

We offer junior and adult private and group lessons, cardio tennis, junior team tennis, as well as monthly mixers and workshops.

We operate as independent contractors under the name of *Central Coast Tennis.* We lease the tennis pro shop and stock tennis merchandise, tennis accessories, strings, balls and racquets. We offer racquet stringing and racquet repair.

The above information was provided by Keith and Darien.

FUN TIMES
AT THE
OLD SMCC CLUBHOUSE

I f you want to know about the fun times in any club, just ask the bartender. In 1981, Danny Hill began tending bar in the old clubhouse on a part-time basis, especially during the three big money-making tournaments: the KFC; the Trefts; and the Produce. Those were VERY busy times. Then SMCC hired him full-time and Danny is still there today.

The old clubhouse really rocked. There was a wooden dance floor and frequently SMCC would hire a local band to play on weekends.

Included here are a few snapshots sure to bring a smile to your face!

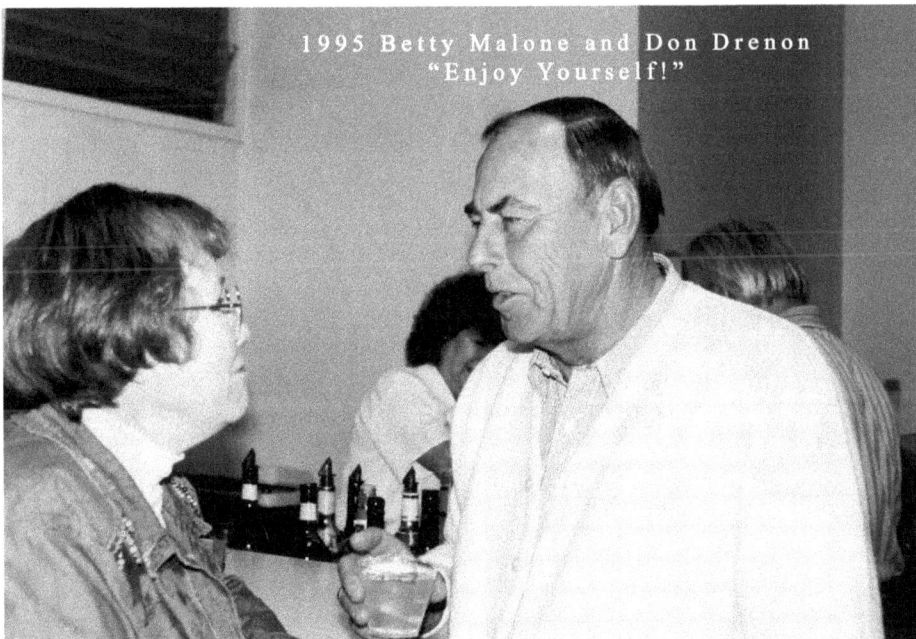

1995 Betty Malone and Don Drenon
"Enjoy Yourself!"

Benny Hill and June Barnett
Super Bowl Party
Other side of shirt reads "I love you"

1994 Fred Quigley and Jane Drenon
"Tell her, Fred"

Christmas Party
Jim and Donna White

Christmas Party
Marty Paulson said
"Everybody get up and Dance!"

Christmas Party
Trish, Danny, June & Marcia

PART 2

CLUB MEMBERS
AND
FAMILIES

FRANK J. McCOY

May 25, 1872 – December 10, 1949

———•◆•———

Frank McCoy came to Santa Maria in 1904 to work for the Union Sugar Plant at Betteravia. He retired in 1915 to pursue his dream – building a world-class inn in Santa Maria. People thought he was crazy. Santa Maria was a small town of about 4,000 people at that time.

He bought property and began construction of his dream inn on the north-south thoroughfare through town. His Santa Maria Inn opened its doors on May 19, 1917. It was quite sensational and Frank knew how to promote it. He had contacts in Hollywood who were attracted to his inn. Word spread and it was a success.

Frank also cultivated local friends. He contributed generously to worthwhile projects in town. For example, he anonymously gifted a new organ to the Methodist church although he was not a member. An individual who was running for a political office tried to take credit for gifting the organ and then Frank disclosed that he was the donor!

When the first meeting of organizers and subscribers for stock in the Santa Maria Golf and Country Club took place, Frank was one of the first 7 subscribers. The meeting took place in the Directors' room of the Bank of Santa Maria on November 16, 1921. Frank was elected President of the Board of Directors of the Santa Maria Country Club.

When Cecil B. DeMille was searching for a place to film *The Ten Commandments,* Frank (and others) convinced him that the Guadalupe Dunes was the ideal spot. This resulted in much publicity and money for nearby Santa Maria.

In 1938, Frank bought the El Encanto Hotel in Santa Barbara. The purchase price is not known, but he sold it for approximately $150,000 in 1943.

Frank had a long-time interest in the advancement of public health work in Santa Barbara County. He was a member of the board of directors of the California Tuberculosis and Health Association from 1939-1942.

When Frank died in 1949, nephew Ed McCoy took over operation of the Santa Maria Inn. Then in September 1962, when Highway 101 opened and north-south freeway traffic no longer flowed by the Santa Maria Inn, guests slowed to a trickle.

FRANK J. McCOY

JAKE L. AND EVELYN WILL

————•◆•————

There probably wouldn't even be a Santa Maria Country Club if it hadn't been for Jake Will. Jake, his wife Evelyn and two children came to Santa Maria in 1941. He initially came here from Columbus, Ohio to survey and lay out Camp Cooke. After completion of that he was hired by S.P. Milling Company to manage a ready-mix operation being set up to supply concrete around-the-clock for building roads, barracks and other facilities at the Camp.

In 1942 Jake moved the ready-mix plant to the Santa Maria Air Base at the corner of Blosser Road and McCoy Lane. It supplied concrete for runways, aprons, and hangars for P-38 fighter planes, and for oilfields, and Santa Maria city growth during and after the war.

Jake became President of SP Milling Company but in 1956 resigned and founded Coast Rock Products. He bought land near town on E. Donovan Road near Suey Park and erected a concrete bridge on the Sisquoc River to mine and process aggregate.

Jake L. Will

Jake was the "behind the scenes" man who approached Dick Weldon and the two of them urged the Board of Directors to take action to purchase the land which was being leased from the Airport District (originally from the County.)

A great deal of work had to be done before purchasing the leased land could become a reality. A bit of history is necessary before we can understand the complexity of events.

The airport lease was a 50-year lease for which the Santa Maria Country Club paid $25 per year plus taxes. The original lease had been made with the County of Santa Barbara, but the ownership of the land had since passed to the Airport District, which meant the Federal Aviation Administration (FAA) had to do an appraisal of the property. The FAA appraisal came in too high so negotiations ensued. The long-term lease held by SMCC was a good negotiating tool and helped bring the price down on the approximately 37 acres. A deal was struck for $160,000.

Numerous changes had come about in past years. Oil had been struck in 1946 on Well #1 on the Santa Maria Country Club property and in 1947 on Well #2. This resulted in "discussions" among the memberships about who should get the royalties from Union Oil. The end result was the formation of a "parent club" and a "playing club," and the writing of new Articles of Incorporation as a nonprofit. Those were filed January 6, 1947.

The formation of the two clubs resulted in two different classes of players. Original stockholders of SMCC stock leased to the playing club for $600 a year plus taxes. The total membership of both classes was 550 members. SMCC purchased back the 100 shares of the original stockholders for $2000 each. Then SMCC sold equity memberships at $1,000 each. Four hundred members bought the new stock, and 150 opted not to buy. The non-equity members could continue on as members but they had to pay $8.00 more per month in dues, and when they left the club their membership was nontransferable.

Jake was a long time member of SMCC and he loved the game of golf. Jake accomplished his goals by working behind the scenes. He was a "working man" and if he saw something that needed to be done he was likely to just roll up his sleeves and do it.

Jake was one of the founders of the Santa Maria Economic Development Association, and he loved Santa Maria. He and Evelyn had two sons, Steve and Jay. Steve and Marie had no children, but Jay had five sons and one daughter. All of Jay's children attended St. Joseph High School where Jay is legendary for his many contributions.

H. STANLEY BROWN

September 21, 1921 — February 29, 1988

———•◆•———

Probably no other member of the Santa Maria Country Club did more to promote golf with the Southern California Golf Association (SCGA) than Stanley Brown. He loved the game of golf, and he was the Board President of SMCC from 1961-1967.

FAMILY HISTORY

Stan's father was Howard C. Brown and Stan had an older brother, Dean Brown. The Brown family had extensive cattle operations in Oregon, California and Texas. Howard teamed up with another brilliant entrepreneur named Silas Sinton. Howard knew the cattle business, and Silas Sinton knew the stockbrokers at Union Sugar. It was the perfect match for forming the Sinton and Brown feedlot near Betteravia and the Union Sugar Plant. Howard moved his family to the Santa Maria area in 1932 to open a cattle feed lot. Young Stanley attended elementary school in Santa Maria, then Santa Maria High School, graduating in 1939. He then went on to UC Davis.

Young Stan had been born in San Francisco. His grandfather, a dairyman, had delivered milk by saddlehorse in San Francisco at the turn of the century. Times were rapidly changing. Howard Brown, who had graduated from UC Davis, was an astute young man. He not only knew the dairy business, he knew the cattle business. He had observed cattle being fed beet pulp at a ranch near Chico.

The Sinton and Brown feedlot grew into a 300-acre spread, one of the world's largest

feedlots. Brown constructed a rail line five miles long which circled the pens, stopping the cars at each pen, where workers filled the troughs with a rich mixture of fermented beet pulp and grains. At its peak, Sinton and Brown feedlots employed 150 people. It was a very efficient operation. Surrounded by fence, all the cattle had to do was eat, drink and poop, which created another problem — what to do with THAT by-product! The solution was to sell it to the fertilizer plants.

Stan was forever an innovator. So that prospective buyers of the fat cattle could view what they were buying without walking around in all that "stuff," in 1954 Stan rescued a San Francisco cable car (#42) from a Bay Area junkyard, restored it, and adapted it to carry cattle buyers out on the rails to see the cattle in the pens.

In August 1979, Sinton and Brown had to shut down. High grain prices, high interest rates, and land prices took their toll. Silas Sinton was dead. Howard Brown had retired. They were losing money rapidly, so the only thing to do was shut down. A colorful era in California history had come to an end. Stan saved his beloved San Francisco Cable Car #42 and moved it to a storage place in Santa Maria. After his death, his widow, Vinnie Lee, gave it to the City of San Francisco for their museum. It was loaded on a cable car trailer and taken on its 300-mile journey up Highway 101 to San Francisco. What a sight that must have been!

STAN'S EARLY LOVE OF AVIATION

After college, Stan set his sights on becoming an airline pilot. When he made up his mind to do something, he pursued it relentlessly. He first became an airline pilot for American Airlines, then Western Airlines. When I asked his daughter why he left being an airline pilot two things had happened. He had met a beautiful airline stewardess by the name of Vinnie Lee Brown.
She didn't even have to change her last name when they got married! And he was needed back in Santa Maria to help his brother and his father with the feedlot operation.

STAN'S LEGACY IN GOLF

Stan served as President of the Santa Maria Country Club from 1961 to 1967. He set about getting SMCC well known in the golfing world and he had the right connections to do so.

Initially, Santa Maria Country Club was almost unknown with the big Southern California Country Clubs. Stan changed all that. He brought influential golfers up to Santa Maria where he entertained them, and introduced them to Santa Maria Country Club hospitality. He not only got himself elected to a seat on the Board of the Southern California Golf Association, he got two other SMCC members (Keith Adams and Tony Cossa) on the board. Stan progressed up the ladder to President of the SCGA in 1970. Then he said to Keith and Tony, "Keep it going," and they did. Keith progressed to President of the SCGA in 1983, and Tony progressed to President of the SCGA in 1996.

Stan sponsored several SMCC golfers to go on golfing trips with him; the most notable of those was a trip to Pine Valley, New Jersey. Dick Weldon, a "Santa Maria born-and bred" boy had probably never been east of the Mississippi before.

He was a member of the prestigious Valley Club in Montecito, California and took quite a few of his SMCC golfing friends to that beautiful club. He lived life to the fullest and was sorely missed when he passed away.

He was influential in getting the California State Open held at the Santa Maria Country Club for a number of years.

On the lighter side, Stan was notorious for pulling pranks on his golfing buddies, and they loved playing with him.

His wife, Vinnie Lee, involved herself with various Santa Maria organizations such as the Minerva Club, golf, etc. She had quite a temper and could hold her own with Stan! They were quite a pair.

According to Stan's obituary he was survived by his widow, Vinnie Lee, his parents, two sons and a daughter, eight grandchildren and a great grandson.

Trolley distributing beet pulp along one of many lines of feeding pens at the Sinton and Brown Feedlot. Although many Santa Marians never saw these feedyards, no one could escape the powerful odors that blew thru Santa Maria from the 1930's to the 1980's when the feedlot closed down. "Fifty Fragrant Years". (Photo courtesy Vennie Lee Brown)

Aerial view SE of huge Sinton & Brown Feedyards in 1950. Town of Betteravia upper right. Lines of SMVRR oil tank cars and sugar beet cars in foreground. Trolley line thruout. (Photo Courtesy Vennie Lee Brown)

RICHARD P. WELDON

———•◆•———

Birthplace: Santa Maria, CA

Education: SMHS Class of 1946
Stanford University, BA,
1950
Stanford University Law
School, JD, 1953

Occupation: Practice of Law, Santa Maria
since 1953

Dick Weldon is a quiet man who doesn't waste time on idle "chit chat." I had never met him, so I dropped by his office around 4 PM on a Wednesday afternoon to set up an appointment to meet with him. I was contemplating writing a book about the Santa Maria Country Club. He said, "I'm in Court the rest of this week so I will have to call you."

Friday afternoon, October 23rd, I received a call: "Dick Weldon. Tomorrow morning, my office 10 a.m."

The next morning, Saturday, October 24, 2015, I arrived promptly in his office. He wasn't in his "court clothes," he was in his "working clothes." Shirt sleeves, no tie, and his hair looked as though he had been running his fingers through it. The picture above bears little resemblance to the man who greeted me. His reading glasses were perched on his nose so he could read, or look at me.

Dick said, "Come on in to the room where all the work gets done around here. His office is an old residence. The dining room has been converted to a "work room." The dining room table and every chair was covered with neat stacks of papers. He said, "Have a seat." I looked at him and merely raised an eyebrow. He said, "OH" and moved the stack of papers to another location. He said, "Let's get started." Again, I just looked at him, as there was no room in front of me to place my writing tablet. He merely took his forearm and scooted a pile of papers over to provide room.

For about an hour and fifteen minutes we worked in fast-paced harmony. He would pull a document or a picture from a stack and ask, "Want that?" If I responded "Yes" (or sometimes YES!!) I would start to latch onto it. He would say, "I have to make a copy of it." Then he would go to the copier, copy it, and then give it back to me.

After a little over an hour he said, "If I come up with any more, I'll give you a call." My brain was on overload with all the wonderful information he had given me. I don't own a briefcase, so I was trying to keep all this material together. He found an old manila folder and said, "Here, use this to keep everything together."

Then Dick relaxed and proudly showed me around his office. He has a huge old picture of Santa Marians which hangs in the entry hallway of his office. It is so old that there are only 3 people in the photo which anyone can identify.

Dick loves history, especially Santa Maria Valley history. He doesn't talk about himself, and I had to "bug" him for a "good" picture for this book. I got the feeling that he is more comfortable with the picture of him which graces this book's cover.

People I have since interviewed indicate that "material possessions" are of little importance to him. For example, Stan Brown (who had plenty of money) gave him a beautiful new golf bag. The next time he and Stan were golfing, he was still carrying his old worn golf bag. Stan asked him where the new bag went. Dick said, "Oh, my son admired that bag so much, I gave it to him."

Seems everyone I knew or interviewed knew Dick Weldon. The listing of offices he has held, and past memberships in civic organizations, fills an entire page. The sporting activities in which he has participated, and excelled, surprised me. One of those made me chuckle: "City of Santa Maria ping pong tournament winner one year." That is a game which requires a high degree of eye/hand coordination!

Dick was on the Stanford University Golf Team — quite an accomplishment since he didn't learn to play golf until he was in college. Dick joined the Santa Maria Country Club in 1953 when he got out of college.

He was a member of the State Elks Championship golf team in 1960 (the same year he was the Exalted Ruler of the Santa Maria Elks Lodge.) Dick was President of the Board of Directors, Santa Maria Country Club in 1989-90.

ANTHONY W. "TONY" AND SUSAN COSSA

———•◆•———

Tony is a 4th generation native of the Santa Maria Valley. His father, T.A. Cossa, became a member of the Santa Maria Country Club in 1947. Initiation fee was $25.00 and dues were $2.00 per month. Tony's mother, "Billee", was also an avid golfer with the Women's Division. Tony's father was also a long-time member of the Santa Maria Elks Lodge, and worked to prepare the Rodeo grounds. He also operated the "roping chute" for many years.

Tony's grandfather emigrated from Switzerland as a young man. He was a dairyman. He took a trip back to Switzerland to find himself a bride, but he didn't have the money to bring her to America.   Ten years later he sent for her and when she arrived they got married. They had 10 children, --- that's a lot of little Cossas! Interesting bit of trivia: Tony's insurance office today is located on a parcel of land that was once a part of his grandfather's dairy land (at the corner of Main Street and Suey Road).

Uncle Charlie Cossa (T.A. Cossa's brother) was also a very active member of the Santa Maria Country Club. In fact, Charlie was one of the many farmers and laborers who took their heavy equipment out and built the "back nine."

When Tony was in the 7th grade (1952), he was one of the kids who took lessons from Frank Hocknell (SMCC's golf pro). Frank gave free lessons to youths during the summer months. Gary Cossa, Tony's older brother, took lessons from Frank as well.

Now another generation of Cossas is very involved in golf at SMCC. Tony's son, Ron, is a very active member who plays regularly at the club.

Tony received a degree in business from the University of Southern California in 1963. In 1983, he successfully passed the examinations and became a Chartered Property/Casualty Underwriter (CPCU).

Tony Cossa began his insurance career joining with Jim Pollard in 1966 to form Pollard & Cossa. In 1986, Pollard & Cossa Insurance Agency was named California Agency of the Year. In 1999, they merged with Bobby Acquistapace to form InWest Insurance. In 2005, InWest merged with Tolman & Wiker Insurance Services.

Tony was a National board member of ACORD, a global nonprofit insurance association. He also served as President of the Independent Insurance Agents Association of Santa Maria; the wine and food society; the Chamber of Commerce (1983); the Santa Maria Valley Economic Development Association (1986); the Rotary Club of Santa Maria (1994); President of the Santa Maria Country Club (1988 & 1999); the Southern California Golf Association (1996); and President of the California Seniors Golf Association (2008). He is past Secretary of the "Vaqueros de Los Ranchos" and served on the Board of Directors of the "Rancheros Visitadores."

Tony Cossa served as Assistant Chairman of the Santa Maria Elks Rodeo Queen contest for 10 years and as Chairman for another 10 years. He also served on the Board of Directors of the Elks Recreation Foundation. He was honored as "Grand Marshal" of the Elks Parade in 1984. He was recognized as "Citizen of the Year" by both the Elks Lodge in 1989 and the Santa Maria Chamber of Commerce in 1991.

Fund-raising endeavors have included: Chairman of the YMCA building fund; Chairman of the first student fund-raising auction "BASH" at St. Joseph's High School; and while president of the Marian Medical Foundation, he chaired the committee that raised funds to build the Marian Heart Center.

Tony helped fund the Central Coast Chapter of "The First Tee," a national organization that focuses on character education for children, and served as its President for five years.

What an amazing multitude of accomplishments he has amassed!

TONY COSSA
PRESIDENT
1987 - 1989

1990's

◆ **1996 - *Tony Cossa*** served at President of the Southern California Golf Association

PATRICK AND JERI FERINI

———•◆•———

Patrick Ferini is a third generation Santa Marian. His father, Milo Ferini, was a farmer. His grandfather emigrated from Switzerland to California in 1880. He was a dairyman and he settled on the Central Coast. Over the years, the dairy industry underwent many changes and improvements. Mechanization made old methods obsolete. Many dairymen left the dairy business and changed vocations. At one time there were 84 dairies on the Central Coast; now they are all gone.

Farming, too, has undergone enormous changes. Specialization and cooperative ventures abound. Cooling plants and refrigeration have improved the delivery time from growers to marketplace to ensure freshness of produce.

It was 1932, ten years before Patrick Ferini was born, that his father, Milo Ferini, and Nick Ardantz, another third generation farmer, joined forces to run a small sugar beet farm near Guadalupe. By 1936, their families had joined the Bonita Packing Company. Sugar beets were replaced with celery, lettuce and other vegetables and a new produce company named Bonipak came into being in the Santa Maria Valley. Today, Bonipak employs more than 600 full-time workers.

Patrick Ferini

Today, eight decades later, the company is still connected to Milo Ferini and Dominick Ardantz, through second-generation owners Milo Ferini, Patrick Ferini and Henry Ardantz, along with third-generation owners Rob Ferini, Mitch Ardantz, Craig Reade, Tom Minetti and Alain Pincot.

Patrick Ferini has been a lifelong member of the Santa Maria Country Club. He remembers riding out on the tractor with his father, Milo, when he was about nine years old where the building of the back nine was taking place. There were a lot of people there with tractors, back-hoes, graders, etc. volunteering their labor and using their equipment.

Years later, Patrick became an avid golfer at the Santa Maria Country Club. He married his wife, Jeri, who was an enthusiastic tennis player, but readily admits that Jeri was a better tennis player than him.

Patrick served as President of the Board of Directors of the Santa Maria Country Club from 1999-2007.

In recent years, health issues have sidelined both Patrick and Jeri from playing either golf or tennis, but they have many years of wonderful memories of great times at the Santa Maria Country Club.

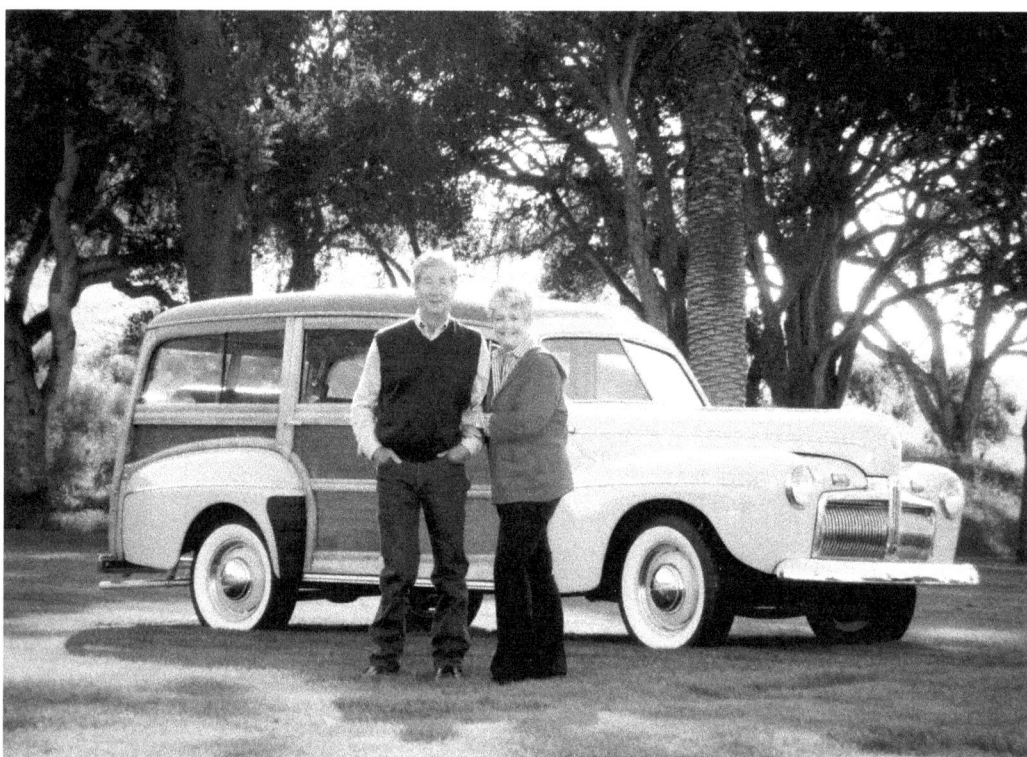

Patrick and Jeri Ferini in front of the classic "Woody," which they restored.

HENRI ARDANTZ

————•◆•————

Henri Pierre Ardantz is a second generation Santa Marian. His father, Juan, was a farmer. His grandfather, Dominick (Nick) Ardantz, emigrated from France in the late 19th century.

It was 1932 when Nick Ardantz and Milo Ferini teamed up to run a small sugar beet farm near Guadalupe, CA , unaware they were setting the stage for an agricultural empire that would one day employ more than 600 full-time workers.

By 1936, their families had joined the Bonita Vegetable Co-op, which eventually became Bonita Packing Company. Sugar beets were replaced with celery, lettuce, and other vegetables. A new produce company, Bonipak, was born in the Santa Maria Valley and still exists today.

Eight decades later, the company is still connected to Dominick Ardantz and Milo Ferini, through second-generation owners Milo Ferini, Patrick Ferini and Henri Ardantz, along with third-generation owners Rob Ferini, Mitch Ardantz, Craig Reade, Tom Minetti and Alain Pincot.

Henri Ardantz is still an active member of the Santa Maria Country Club, and in the past, served on the Board of Directors for several years.

Included herein are six rare and historic pictures showing progression of Bonita Packing and Betteravia Farms. The earliest one is dated 1955. I especially like the one of the three Bonita Packing Directors dated 1985 (30 years later). Patrick Ferini looks incredibly young, with his "Beatles" style haircut!

When I met with Henri on Friday, June 10, 2016 at Bonipak, he introduced me to his son Mitchell. Time was very limited as they were both leaving to attend Mitch's son's graduation. Then Henri was leaving a couple of days later for a brief vacation. Then in July, Henri was leaving for his first-ever REAL vacation. He had celebrated his 80th birthday on May 22 and decided it was time to do some traveling. He and his younger brother, Michael, who lives in San Jose, were taking three weeks and seeing some of this beautiful country. God bless you, Henri!

Below: Bonita Packing
Co. 700 blk. S. Blosser
Rd. — mid 1970's. (Photo
courtesy Henri Ardantz)

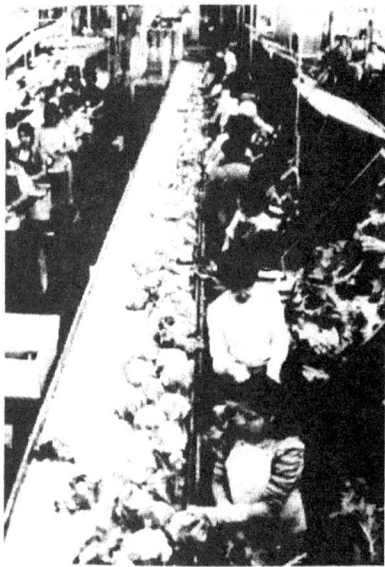

Traditional cauliflower packing lines —
Bonita Packing — mid 1970's. (Photo courtesy Henri Ardantz)

Bonita Packing Directors — 1985. *L-R:* Henri
Ardantz, Patrick Ferini, Milo Ferini. (Photo
courtesy Henri Ardantz)

Mechanical loading of lettuce boxes — Betteravia farms early 1980's.
(Photo courtesy Henri Ardantz)

Right: Mobile cauliflower
harvester-packer pro-
duces boxes ready for
cooler and market —
early 1990's. (Photo courtesy Henri Ardantz)

Below: Bonita Packing
Co. 700 blk. S. Blosser
Rd. — mid 1970's. (Photo
courtesy Henri Ardantz)

DON "DONNIE" AND PHYLLIS MUNOZ

———— •◆• ————

I had never heard the name "Munoz" until Don Drenon spoke it in answer to a question I asked him. Don and Jane were sitting on the patio at the Country Club having a drink where Don could smoke. I knew Don had played in the "Portuguese Club" on Thursdays for a long time, so I asked, "How many of the old-timers still play in the club?" Don raised one finger and said, "Munoz." It seems everyone, except me, at the Santa Maria Country Club knew Donnie Munoz!

The holidays, health issues, etc. intervened, and I didn't get back to working on the book for quite some time. On May 9, 2016 I was able to get an interview with Donnie.

Parents: Frank and Gladys Munoz, who were born and raised in Nipomo. They married in June 1923 and relocated to Santa Maria, where they were blessed with three children (two boys and then a girl.) The oldest boy was Bill, then two years later was Donnie, then Rosalie.

Frank opened up a Union Oil service station at 629 S. Broadway in 1935, which turned out to be a good location. Donnie was 9 years old and his brother, Bill, was 11 years old. They were in awe of all the movie stars and their fancy cars that frequented the nearby Santa Maria Inn. Years later, they opened two more Union stations, one in Santa Maria and one in Orcutt. Frank, Bill and Donnie formed a partnership.

You need to remember what a tremendous job it was to own and operate a service station in those days. You didn't just pump gas. Many of those stations had a mechanic who repaired cars, patched tires, etc. Kids were often given a job washing windshields, checking the oil, putting air in your tires, and cleaning the restroom (UGH)!

Donnie graduated in mid-term 1943 from Santa Maria High School and enlisted in the Navy, and spent the remainder of World War II as a radio operator on a destroyer. Then in 1950, he got called back into the military service (Navy). A week before he shipped out, he married his sweetheart, Phyllis Kyle.

Sixty-six years later, Phyllis and Donnie are still married, have 4 kids, 6 grandkids, and 4 great-grandkids. All four of their children still live in Santa Maria. At age 90, Donnie cherishes every day and still is able to play golf out at the Santa Maria Country Club where he has been a member since 1950. His father and his brother also enjoyed many rounds of golf at SMCC.

Donnie was able to fill in a number of gaps in the Santa Maria Country Club History. He says it is true that there are P-38s buried under the 14th fairway. Hancock Field was a flight training facility during World War II.

As you read this book you will notice numerous places where Donnie was able to identify people in very old photos, etc. I am so fortunate to have his input.

"VION" DIXON

Photo courtesy of Tony Cossa

The above photo reflects some of the good times had at the second clubhouse building. Donnie Munoz was able to identify the event, but not the exact date, when the old photo was taken. It was a celebration during one of "Chicken Charlie's " tournaments at the Santa Maria Country Club in which a dozen or so Hawaiian golfers flew over to compete.

Vion was an incredible cocktail waitress, in the 1960s and 1970s, and she had a "photographic memory." When you walked into the bar she not only recognized you, she remembered what you usually ordered to drink.

Charlie Vest owned two Kentucky Fried Chicken (KFC) franchises in Santa Maria, one in San Luis Obispo, one in Arroyo Grande, and probably more, in the 60s and 70s, thus his fellow golfers at SMCC nicknamed him "Chicken Charlie." Notice the two photos in the Women's Division chapter where Charlie Vest is pictured, and in the other photo Sally Scaroni is shown accepting the KFC trophy in 1971.

Charlie Vest also organized a group of SMCC golfers and their wives to fly to Hawaii and play in tournaments there. Donnie Munoz and his wife, Phyllis, went on that trip. Donnie said he didn't win any trophies, but they had the time of their lives.

The "VION" picture is a piece of history in another way. Donnie Munoz identified the band in the background as the Omer Meeker Band (all local boys):

1. Julius Cardoza is playing the trombone.
2. Fred Homann is playing the piano. He was a CPA that worked for Cal City Water.
3. Henry Neiggemann is playing the drums —he is just a faint shadow (barely visible) in the background on the left side of the microphone stand.
4. Joe Brass, who was their trumpet player is not in the photo.

If the picture had shown the bar, you might have seen Bill Ferrell tending bar. He was Rosalie (Munoz) Ferrell's husband. He also played golf at the Santa Maria Country Club.

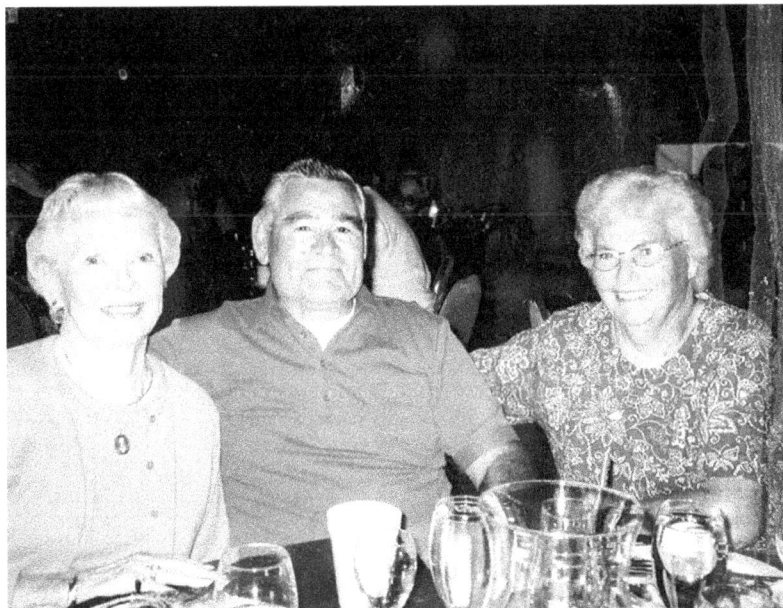

L to R: Sally Scaroni, Donnie Munoz, and Phyllis Munoz.

DEAN "DINO" AND MABEL COLLI

---◆---

Dino's father, Silvio Colli, emigrated from Dervio, Italy around the turn of the century. He was a dairy farmer and already had a brother here who had a dairy farm near Lompoc. Silvio and his brother joined forces in the dairy business.

Young hard-working Italian men from Italy get homesick and lonely. Not only that, their cooking for their hired hands left much to be desired! Silvio thought of Bea Dittamintico back in Dervio, Italy. He wrote to her and asked her if she would come to America and cook for him, his brother, and the hired hands. Bea wrote back and said, "Only if you marry me first. Then I will come!"

Such an arranged marriage seems strange to us today, but it was not uncommon in 1900. Bea arrived, they got married, and the picture below, taken in 1929, shows the results. Dino was 10 years younger than his siblings.

Front Row: Silvio, Dean, Bea (Dittamintico) Colli.
Second Row: Elsie (Colli) Rezzonico; Joe Colli; Arthur Colli; Sylvia (Colli) Cheswick.

Dino's early life was a hard-working one but one where all the family pitched in and helped each other. Dino was drafted into the Army when World War II broke out, but he never was actively involved in any combat duty.

When World War II ended and he returned home to civilian life, he met a beautiful girl by the name of Mabel Denman. Her mother had died when Mabel was about six years of age. Her father, Charles, was left with four older boys and six-year-old Mabel. Fortunately, an aunt by the name of Marian St. Claire took her in and lovingly raised her as if her own child. Otherwise, she would probably have ended up in an orphanage.

Dino and Mabel were married in St. Mary's Catholic Church in Santa Maria on August 23, 1946, and will celebrate their 70th wedding anniversary this year. Dino will be 90 years young on 9/11/16 and Mabel will be 90 on 10/27/16. They joined the Santa Maria Country Club on June 1, 1962, and both began playing golf immediately. Mabel played for 10 years. Dino still plays on Tuesdays, Thursdays and Saturdays and usually scores lower than his age — quite an accomplishment for a 90-year-old.

When Vandenberg Air Force Base was founded, the Colli dairy farm, along with other farm land that was located within the boundary of the new base, was acquired by the Government under the power of eminent domain. The Colli family accepted the money received and purchased a much smaller dairy farm east of Santa Maria.

The three Colli brothers entered into a partnership in a business called *Dino's Deli* on E. Main Street in Santa Maria after the dairy farm went out of business. Dino is the lone survivor of the Colli siblings.

Dean and Mabel Colli

MILTON SR. AND EVELYN GUGGIA

———•◆•———

If anyone thinks growing up on a dairy farm is easy, they don't know their history. This story focuses on one branch of the huge family of Guggias who emigrated from Switzerland to build a new life in America.

Milt's uncle, John Guggia, came to America from San Antonino, Switzerland in 1890. His brother, Peter, followed in 1901. The two brothers were employed by area dairymen, enabling them to save their earnings. In 1907, the two brothers were able to start their own dairy partnership on leased property, just south of Pismo Beach where the Quarterdeck Restaurant now sits.

John Guggia returned to Switzerland in 1909 to marry Maria, and they returned to America in 1910. They continued to operate the dairy until 1911, when Peter also returned to Switzerland to find a wife. He married a young lady by the name of Domenica Bognuda.

They were married in Switzerland and returned to California in 1914 while Domenica was with child. The couple went on to have seven children: Lucio, Lawrence, Martha, Betty, Vernon, Lydia and Milt.

Having two families under one roof was too crowded. John and Peter decided to dissolve the partnership and continue

Milt, Sr. and Evelyn Guggia

to do business on their own. The way they split the herd was rather unique. They selected the cows alternately, much like children pick a kickball team on a playground, with Uncle John picking a cow first, then my dad would pick one, etc.

Uncle John then rented a ranch in Cayucos. Peter and Domenica leased property known as "The Biddle Ranch" located just west of what is now Lopez Lake. They operated at this location until 1927. Then my folks purchased an 800 acre ranch which is where the Laeticia Vineyard is now located just south of Arroyo Grande. They moved their livestock by herding them through the upper Arroyo Grande valley and down U.S. 101 to the new ranch. No moving trucks were used. Their children now numbered seven, Lucio, Lawrence, Martha, Betty, Vernon, Lydia and Milt, were moved by wagon. The family remained there until 1934 when Milt moved the dairy to leased property on Bonita School Road.

In 1947, my parents (Peter and Domenica) retired to a ranch they had purchased on Black Road. My brother, Vernon, and I formed a partnership and continued as Guggia Dairy. It remained at this site until 1979, when the dairy was dissolved and all the cows were sold.

Let's flash back to Milt and Evelyn. They were married in 1949 in Las Vegas, Nevada. Evelyn's maiden name was Reed. They proceeded to have four children: Milt Jr., Gary, Vickie and Traci.

Son Gary partnered with Uncle Lucio and remained in farming. It is Gary who is carrying on the farming tradition in the family. Gary now owns a successful trucking company with 12 trucks, called *Guggia Trucking.* He and his wife, Chris (Dickson) Guggia, have three children: Domenic, Damion and Justine.

Traci has remained in the area and is very involved in family history. Much of the material in this article was recorded on paper by Traci. She has worked for her brother in the restaurant business since its inception as MGE.

Vickie went away to college, and worked as an airline stewardess for TWA for 15 years. She returned to Santa Maria when the health of her father began to fail. Evelyn (Vickie's mom) had passed away on April 20, 2012. Vickie is married to Kevin Galvin, and has two children, Matthew and Laura.

Milt Guggia, Sr.

Milt Jr. and his wife, Angel (Ardizone) Guggia, are in the restaurant business. They have three daughters: Missy, Krista and Kacie, who all three joined the SMCC Tennis Club in 1994.

Long before owning restaurants, Milt Jr. started out owning and operating ONE catering truck in Santa Maria. It was called *Pate's Catering.* According to his oldest daughter, Missy, he would get up before dawn and head off for work, returning late in the evening. The three little girls did not have a "set bedtime." Mom would let them stay up until their dad got home.

Pate's Catering did well. When he had expanded to six trucks, he sold the business and opened his first restaurant, *The Jetty.*

Today, the Guggia family owns and operates several excellent restaurants. They recently opened a new one in Santa Maria called *Crumbles.* Granddaughter, Missy, manages it. Until failing health precluded him from doing so, Milt Sr. helped his son at the restaurants. At first, Milt Sr. helped at various jobs around the restaurant, but as his son acquired additional restaurants his role focused on supervising and helping keep the landscaping pristine. And what a great job he did in that capacity. Their restaurants provide employment for many people and contribute much to the economy of the Santa Maria area.

Nearly all of the Guggias over the years have been active members of the Santa Maria Country Club, not only in golf, but also in tennis. In the Women's Division chapter of this book I noticed a picture of a Virginia Guggia taken by Sally Scaroni circa 1954 when women golfers were required to wear long skirts!

Martha (Guggia) Vanetti (Milton's sister) was very involved in SMCC golf and was very active in the Women's Division in the early 60s. Her daughter, Rosemarie, was the Junior Club Champion in September 1967. Rosemarie (Vanetti) Bullock is married to Bob Bullock and still lives in Santa Maria.

SEPTEMBER 1967

Jr. Club Champion Rosemarie Vanetti, right; Susan Dutton, left

Milton, Sr. and Peter ("Papa") Guggia

HARVEY "KEITH" AND SANDY ADAMS
February 8, 1925 — November 3, 2015

———•◆•———

Keith Adams was born in 1925 in Glendive, Montana and was the fourth son of a farming family of eight. He graduated from Dawson County High School in 1942 and after a short stint with Safeway stores, he enlisted in the U. S. Navy to serve his country in World War II. He worked as a Storekeeper aboard ship, which took him around the world, first to the South Pacific, New Caledonia, the Hawaiian Islands, Iwo Jima (where he observed the raising of the American Flag on Mount Suribachi), and even to Siberia. During the invasion of Okinawa, his ship was struck by a suicide boat, which caused severe damage but survived the attack. Proving it is a small world, Keith was transported to New Caledonia on a ship that had Santa Maria Country Club member Leroy MacDonald as a crew member.

Keith was discharged in 1946 on his 21st birthday and joined his mother in Burbank, CA, where he enrolled in Sawyer Business School and graduated in 1948 with a degree in Business Administration, and earned his public accounting license. While working for a CPA in Glendale he worked with Radco as one of the company's clients. Radco saw his talent and hired him in 1949. The firm relocated to Santa Maria in 1956 where he was promoted

Keith and Sandy Adams in 2012

to General Manager. Another SMCC member, John MacGregor, was the Plant Superintendent. Together they purchased the company in 1966, and operated the business for 22 years, selling it in 1988.

Keith joined Santa Maria Country Club in 1956 and became active in tournaments and handicapping. Obviously, before computers, he had to calculate handicaps manually, which he did for nearly five years before being elected to the Board in 1960, serving as President in 1969 and 1970. In 1970 Keith, brothers Jack & Jim O'Keefe, and Stan Brown purchased Rancho Maria Golf Course where he served on the corporate board for 42 years. While serving as president in 1970, Keith, Jake Will, Dick Weldon, Maurice Twitchell, Tony Cossa and Jack O'Keefe developed a plan to form a new club, known as the Player's Club. Part of this plan included the acquisition of the property west of the railroad tracks from the Airport District. Keith was called upon again to serve on the Board of Directors of SMCC in 1980, serving a second stint as president in 1983-1984.

Keith Adams in 1983, as president of the SCGA, presents winner's trophy to Dave Hobby.

Keith's golf organization experience didn't stop at SMCC. He served as a committeeman and chairman of the California State Open for some 15 years, which was conducted at SMCC for many years. The last Open was held at SMCC in 1978. While serving in this capacity he was joined by other SMCC members: Fred & Connie Quigley; Meg Smith (Bryn's mother); Jack O'Keefe and Tony Cossa.

At the urging of Stan Brown (SMCC president in the late 1950s and early 1960s), Keith became active as a committeeman with the SCGA, which led to his election to the Southern California Golf Association (SCGA) board in 1970 on which he remained for 15 years, serving as the SCGA President in 1983 and another year as Past President.

Keith also was a board member of the California Golf Association (CGA), an amateur golf organization, in 1980, and served as the CGA board president in 1984. The CGA held the California Amateur Championship tournament at Pebble Beach, which he played more times than he could count — for free, and served as a referee for years. During this stint, he had the pleasure of meeting "up-and-comers" Mark O'Meara, Corey Pavin and Duffy Waldorf, names we are familiar with today as PGA Tour players and winners.

A SPECIAL NOTE: The Santa Maria Country Club is one of only a handful of clubs to have the honor of seeing three SCGA presidents — Stan Brown in 1970, Keith Adams in 1983, and Tony Cossa in 1996.

JOHN AND MARGE MacGREGOR

———— • ◆ • ————

John MacGregor was born July 5, 1921 on Prince Edward Island, Canada. Marge (Jones) MacGregor was born June 23, 1923 in Victoria, Canada. Above is the wedding picture of Marge's parents, Frida Kristjanson and Joseph George Jones. The picture was probably taken in 1913. Marge's mother was born in Iceland (date unknown) and her father was born in Wales (date unknown.) Marge's mother, in the picture, is the tiny lady in the dark attire holding the bouquet of flowers. Her father, standing next to her mother, is in his Royal Canadian Mounted Police uniform. He drove a 13-dog sled team in the Canadian wilderness and was often gone for six weeks at a time. Canadian winters are fierce, with blizzards often occurring unexpectedly. The jail, where Frida lived while Joseph was gone, is somewhere in the background behind where the minister is standing.

The people on the left side of the photograph are Eskimos, and there were probably a few Cree Indians in attendance since a wedding was a big occasion in this lonely land. The banners waving overhead proclaim the happy occasion.

Fast forward to 1943. John and Marge were married on October 16, 1943 in Winnipeg, Manitoba, Canada. It was the middle of World War II (England and Canada were already in the war far ahead of the United States.) John was in the Royal Canadian Air Force, and was on a VERY brief leave. Times were really tough for everyone and these young newlyweds were no exception. Marge had sewn her own dress for the occasion, and he had his Air Force uniform. Their wedding night was spent in a run-down hotel with a "shared" bathroom down the hall. When Marge made her way to the bathroom a very drunken man exited the bathroom and nearly collided with her! There were no restaurants in the vicinity, so they ate what food they had with them in their room which turned out to be wieners and tiny donuts! Their wedding picture is shown above.

John and Marge's Wedding Day, October 16, 1943.

The war ended and John returned home to Canada. The war had taken its toll on the economy and Canada was no exception. Jobs were scarce or nonexistent. To complicate things even more, in 1947 to their joy, a baby boy, Wayne MacGregor arrived on the scene.

They struggled for about five years to make ends meet and finally John came home and said, "Let's move to the United States." Marge said, "O.K." Thus began the long, tedious process of making their dream a reality. Endless paperwork. Finding a sponsor. Health questionnaires. TB and smallpox shots. And then the most crucial issue of all, "Do you have a job when you get to the U.S.?" John had to tell a bit of a little white lie, as he responded, "I'm going to start my own business." Actually, years later he did start his own business.

I asked John how long he had spent in the Royal Canadian Air Force. He responded, "Four years, three months, four days and three hours!"

John had a lot of talent and he worked at various jobs when he arrived in Pasadena, then finally landed a job with RADCO. In 1953, the MacGregors were blessed with a second son, Warren.

John worked for RADCO in Pasadena where he advanced to Plant Superintendent. In 1956, when RADCO decided to relocate its business to Santa Maria, California, John was offered the job of Plant Manager. Another RADCO employee, Keith Adams, was offered the job of General Manager in Santa Maria. Ten years later (1966) John and Keith formed a partnership and purchased the company. They owned and operated RADCO for 22 years, and sold the business in 1988.

Both Marge and son, Warren, were excellent golfers. In 1975, Marge won Women's Club Champion and in that same year Warren won Men's Club Champion. Warren won that same honor several times. To the right, is a picture of Marge and her son, Warren, which appeared in the Santa Maria Times in 1975.

Marge and son, Warren.

John and Marge joined Santa Maria Country Club in 1958 and are still active in the club. They have many warm memories of the old clubhouse (second building, rebuilt after the fire) and loaned me some snapshots taken on the day of demolition. The cardboard "targets" in the windows on the right end of the building were used for guys to fire golf balls at, and John was the first guy to hit the center of a target. That end of the building was where the wooden dance floor was located.

FOOTNOTE

John passed away August 25, 2016 with his loving family at his side. He left a legacy that few could emulate. He had been an active 50-year member of First Christian Church, having served as both a deacon and elder.

WILLIAM E. AND BETTY A. COUEY

—·◆·—

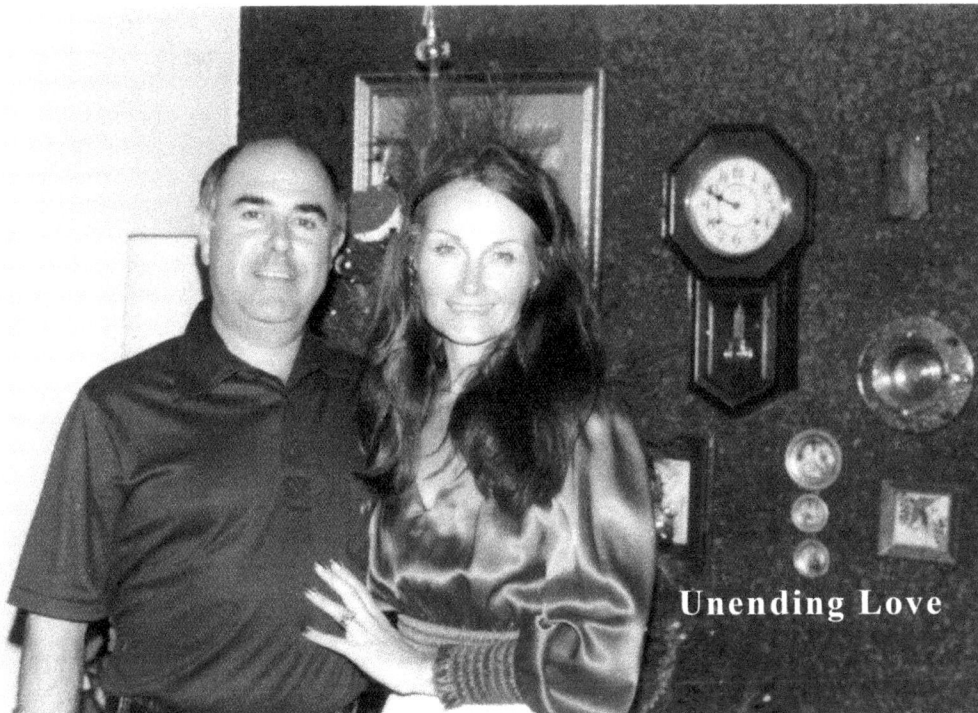

Unending Love

Bill Couey was born January 15, 1932 in San Francisco, California. He grew up in Benecia, California where he attended high school, then attended San Jose State, where he received his degree in Education, then went on to get his master's degree. He and Betty were high school sweethearts at Benecia High School. He was a couple of years ahead of her in school.

Betty was born in Maquoketa, Iowa. She was an only child, and her mother was a school teacher. Her father's employment required them to move from time to time, so she received a lot of history lessons in her early life.

Bill and Betty were married on July 11, 1954. Bill's first job after getting his degree was as Principal of Main Street School in Santa Maria. It has long since been torn down, but it was located where the Wells Fargo Bank now stands, at the corner of Main and Miller. Bill loved his job, he loved the kids and they loved him back. Many times during the course of writing this book I have heard, "He was the most wonderful Principal we ever had." Bill loved the game of golf and served as President, SMCC Board of Directors. He and Betty also loved the game of tennis.

Bill and Betty were blessed with one daughter who lives in Santa Maria. She is a joy and comfort to them. They celebrated 62 years of marriage on July 11, 2016.

FRED AND CONNIE QUIGLEY

———•◆•———

Fred was born December 20, 1934 in Camden, New Jersey. He joined the U. S. Air Force in 1954, and his career brought him to Vandenberg Air Force Base in 1961. There he met a beautiful girl by the name of Connie Centeno who was a civil service employee for the Air Force in their budget office. It was love at first sight, and they got married in a civil ceremony in 1961. Since she was Catholic they got married again in Saint John Newman Catholic Church in Santa Maria!

Connie Centeno was born November 15, 1932 in Gonzales, California. Her folks moved to Casmalia, California when she was four years old where she attended elementary school, then attended and graduated from Santa Maria High School. She then began her career with Civil Service at Vandenberg.

The Quigleys have four children: Cynthia, Gary, Ruben, and Fred, Jr. The family joke is that when dad dies, young Fred will no longer be a "Junior"!

I had mistakenly thought that the Quigley Cup tournament played every third week in October was sponsored by Fred and Connie, but Fred says that is not the case; the Santa Maria Country Club sponsors it. Fred and Connie joined the Santa Maria Country Club in 1969 and have been active members ever since. They bought a membership in the Tennis Club before the courts were ever built, as they both played tennis.

DAVID L. AND DEE PRATER

————•◆•————

Dave and Dee Prater

Dave was born June 15, 1934 in Excelsior Springs, Missouri. Due to his father's employment, his family relocated several times. In Kansas City, Missouri at the age of 12, his folks discovered their son had a very special talent ... he was a gifted pianist. They provided him with lessons and he has retained that talent to this day. What an amazing gift!

His family moved to Neosho, Missouri where Dave attended high school and graduated in 1952. He then went on to college at the University of Arkansas, worked his way through on his own, and graduated in 1958.

Dave then got a job with U. S. Civil Service and worked at Norton Air Force Base in San Bernardino, California. It was there he met Dee Adams, a native Californian who was a talent in her own right. At the age of 9, her artistic talent was discovered by a friend and neighbor who purchased a piece of her art work. She started out working with oil paintings, but then progressed to sculpting in bronze.

These two talented people got married on July 9, 1964 and Dave secured a job at Vandenberg Air Force Base. They joined the Santa Maria Country Club in 1966, and are still loyal members today. Their son, Todd, won the Santa Maria Country Club championship in 1983.

Dave at the piano.

Adrenaline Rush

Artist Dee at work.

PETER SAMUEL STEFONI

December 29, 1925 — May 16th, 2016

———•◆•———

Peter was a member of the Santa Maria Country Club for nearly 50 years, and he loved the game of golf. It was not unusual for him to play over 240 rounds of golf in a year.

Peter was born in Tacoma, Washington. During high school, he worked at Todd Shipyard, making aircraft carriers, victory ships and transports.

In 1944, he joined the U.S. Navy where he worked as a typist. After World War II ended, in 1946 he was honorably discharged and moved back to Tacoma. He worked in the wholesale produce business and attended Seattle University. While at a dance, Pete met Garnett Rivette and they married in 1946. During this time his grandmother, aunt and uncle moved to Los Angeles. Pete worked for his uncle at John B. Greco Produce Company.

While in Los Angeles, Pete and Garnett had four children: Steven, Karen, John Peter and Susan. It was also in Los Angeles that he became a huge fan of the Dodgers, Lakers and Rams.

In 1963, Pete and his family moved to Santa Maria, California, where he opened Peter Stefoni Company, broker of fresh fruits and vegetables.

Pete loved to sing and dance, especially to "Big Band" music such as Benny Goodman and Tommy Dorsey; he enjoyed opera and classic movies; and he was competitive in table tennis. Pete's true loves were family and golf. And his family loved him back. He was truly blessed.

One Wednesday evening, many months ago, we invited Pete to join us for dinner at Atari-Ya. We offered to pick him up but he said his daughter, Susan, could bring him. They arrived shortly after we got there. I asked Susan if she had any trouble finding the place, and suddenly Keiko, the owner, came over and gave Susan a great big hug. All four of us had a good laugh over that! Susan's husband is Japanese.

Two days before he passed away when we were visiting Pete at Marian Extended Care, Pete said, "Do you know my grandson plays the drums?" We did, and had heard him play. There was such pride in his voice. He loved music so much. He also said to me, "I think I could tell you some good stories now." About that time his physical therapist arrived so we had to leave. I never got to hear those good stories.

Pete had a very special long-time friendship with Al and Pat Portlock. The Portlocks have been members of the Santa Maria Country Club since April 1981.

JOHN AND BARBARA EGGERT

———•◆•———

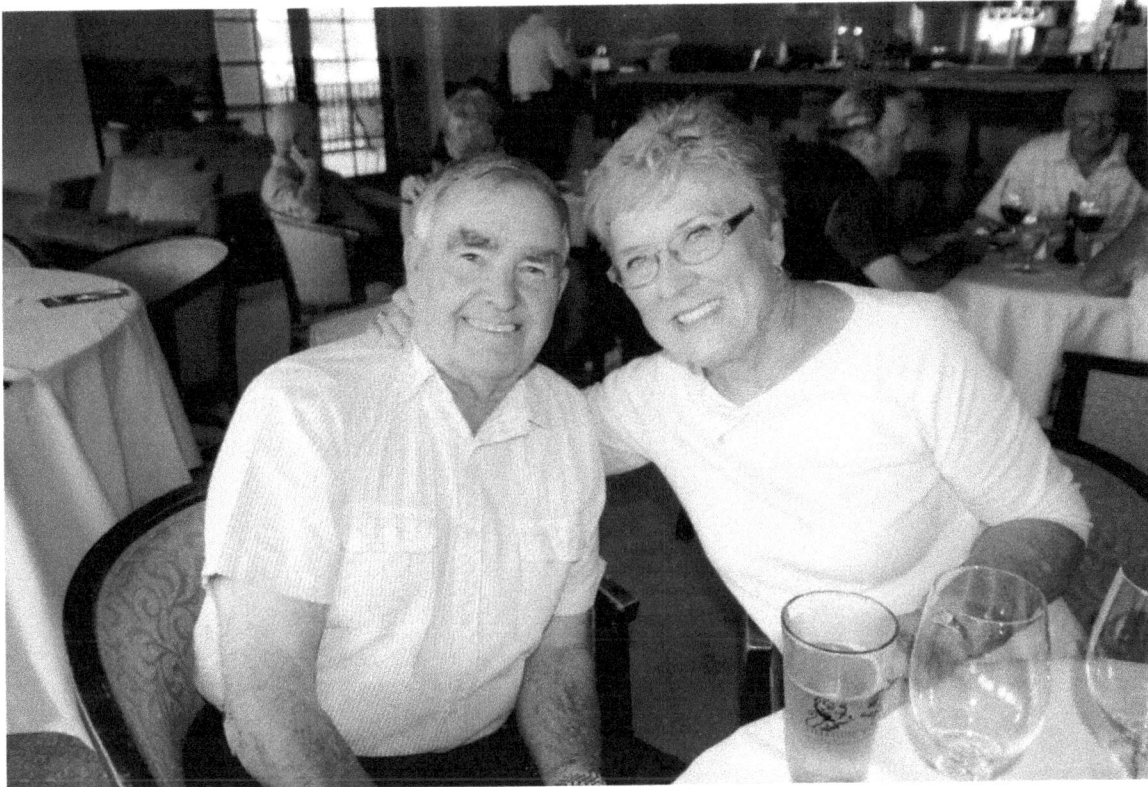

John was born in Newport Beach, California. After high school he went to Orange Coast College. A job offer brought him to Santa Maria in 1969, and he loved both Santa Maria and his new job at Coast Counties Warehouse. He and the owner worked well together, and when the owner retired, John bought the business. He still owns Coast Counties Warehouse today.

Barbara was born in Cleveland, Ohio. Her family moved to Redlands, California when she was five years old. After high school she went to the University of Redlands and got her teaching credentials. She came to Santa Maria to interview for a teaching job and was hired. She was 22 years of age. Her first school was Oakley Elementary School which was near the farmland. She worried about the kids when the crop dusting planes came swooping down very low to spray the nearby fields.

Barbara's next teaching job was at Alvin Elementary School. There the odor from nearby Williams feed lots was pretty bad until the feed lots were closed. Her next school was Ontiveros. During the course of her teaching career, she taught third, fifth and sixth grades. She said probably her favorite grade to teach was fifth grade.

John and Barbara joined the Santa Maria Country Club in 1969. John's work schedule was more flexible, so he was able to play golf in the early years of their membership. During the course of her teaching career Barbara had very little time to play golf, but when she retired she became an excellent golfer. In fact, Barbara had her first-ever hole in one on #16 in August 2016.

CHUCK AND EVELYN PORTMAN

———— • ◆ • ————

Chuck and Evelyn Portman,
LADIES INVITATIONAL, Santa Maria Country Club, October 13, 2015

Very few couples can handle the stress of juggling careers, raising children, being successful business partners, and keeping a marriage together. Anyone who says it is easy is lying. But let me introduce you to a Santa Maria Country Club couple who has managed to do just that:

Chuck Portman, born November 7, 1939, in Butler, Pennsylvania.
Evelyn Portman, born February 23, 1941, in Merced, California.

These two met in Southern California and got married July 15, 1967. The Portmans purchased *Dieno's Draperies, Inc.* in 1974 and Chuck moved to Santa Maria in October 1974, soon followed by Evelyn in the winter of 1975.

They joined the Santa Maria Country Club, and became very active in both tennis and golf. The tennis courts didn't open until 1977. Chuck and Evelyn were one of the first couples to purchase a tennis club membership.

Chuck and Evelyn owned *Dieno's Draperies, Inc.* and worked side-by-side there until the "big box" stores came to Santa Maria and family businesses were no longer able to compete. The Portmans decided to retire at the end of 1995.

The Portmans went into real estate and formed Portman Realty. There they again worked side-by-side, Chuck as the Broker, and Evelyn as the "jack of all trades" (or should I say Jill?) in the office. Finally, at the age of 70, Chuck retired and closed Portman Realty.

What an asset these two have been to the Santa Maria Country Club. They no longer play tennis, but both are still active golfers. Their son, Mike Portman, is currently (2016) the Senior Club Champion, and his mother, Evelyn, is the Santa Maria Country Club Senior Women's Net Champion. Golf excellence seems to run in the family!

MIKE AND PAT GAUGHEN

Photo courtesy of Keith Natzke

This special couple moved to Santa Maria in June 1981, and joined the Santa Maria Country Club in July 1981.

Pat was born in Rolette, North Dakota. It's a humorous story how she ended up marrying Mike in Denver Colorado. She and some of her girlfriends decided the "pickings were pretty lean" for husbands in North Dakota so they moved to Denver to find "rich" husbands! She met Mike, he wasn't rich, but they fell in love, got married and had five children (four girls and one boy.)

Mike was born in Schuyler, Nebraska. After graduating from high school, he went to Denver and attended University of Colorado — Denver Extension Center where he graduated in 1957 with a degree in electrical engineering. He was hired by Martin-Marietta.

In June 1981, he obtained a promotion to Vandenberg Air Force Base where he eventually became Director/Operations Manager for the Peacekeeper Missile Program.

Both Mike and Pat have enjoyed these many years at the Santa Maria Country Club. Mike still plays several times a week, but admits his golf scores are not what they once were. Pat had to give up playing golf not long ago, but she still comes out to dinner and social functions at the club.

They are going on a long road trip to: Las Vegas, Nevada; Denver, Colorado; Schuyler, Nebraska; and Chatfield, Minnesota where there will be a family reunion of Pat's family. Bon voyage and a safe return to Santa Maria!

GARY AND SANDI JOHNSON

—— • ◆ • ——

Gary was born and raised in Santa Maria. His parents were Clyde and Oma Johnson. He has one sibling, Norma Seaman, who still resides in Santa Maria. Their parents are both deceased. Gary graduated from Santa Maria High School in 1957, then went on to the University of the Pacific in Stockton on a full football scholarship. He graduated in 1961 with a major in Physical Education. His father died in 1962, and he returned to Santa Maria.

Sandi Garrison was born in Akron, Ohio. After graduating from high school, she went on to Kent State University where she majored in Education and received her teaching credentials. She and five other young graduates came out to Santa Maria seeking employment. She got a job teaching fourth grade at Miller School. After other teaching assignments, she eventually became Principal of Miller School and retired from the very school where she had started.

Gary and Sandi both have a wonderful sense of humor. I asked where they met. Both laughed and said, "We met in *The Attic.*" They proceeded to tell me about this "watering hole" where young singles hung out after work. Sandi and some of her girlfriends were there and this cute guy named Gary came in. Because he worked for Hunt Foods they thought he was a member of the famous J.B. Hunt family!!

To make a long story short, Gary and Sandi got married on September 8, 1962. They proceeded to have two sons, Eric and Derron. Financially, times were a little tough. Sandi kept on teaching, and Gary had various jobs. Gary decided to pursue a teaching degree at Cal Poly. He not only attained that goal, he went on — all the while still working — and obtained his master's degree from Cal Poly.

In 1992, this busy, hard-working couple was finally able to join the Santa Maria Country Club and take up golf, a game at which they now excel. Sandi is also busy at the club, taking on volunteer jobs such as President of the Women's Division in 2010-11.

Keeping up with what is going on in the lives of their six grandchildren, ranging in age from two to 28 years of age, also keeps them busy.

Gary and Sandi just celebrated 54 years of marriage. Congratulations, you two!

RONALD AND MARCIA EDWARDS

Do you think Ron and Marcia learned to do the hula in Hawaii?

Both Ron and Marcia were born and raised in Niagara Falls, New York. They got engaged the night of their high school prom and they were married August 12, 1967, and Ron joined the Navy. He is a Viet Nam veteran and he was stationed in Honolulu for three years. Marcia worked for Civil Service at the base while there. Ron's work while in the Navy was as an air crew electrician.

They moved to Santa Maria in August 1970, where Ron attended Hancock College, then Cal Poly, graduating with a teaching degree in Industrial Arts. Marcia worked (always) as a bookkeeper and as a "working team" they managed to survive the lean years.

At first, after college, Ron taught 7th and 8th grades; he hated it! It would only take one unruly or undisciplined kid to ruin his day. After three months he quit and started working as a Union Journeyman Carpenter. In 1979, he went into business for himself and in 1982 he built his first subdivision. He went on to build 14 subdivisions.

The name of his company is *Sculptures By Edwards.* Marcia has worked alongside him as his bookkeeper. He built Edwards Community Center and donated it to the City of Santa Maria.

They have two boys, both born at Marian in Santa Maria. Phillip was born in 1973, and was on the Santa Maria Tennis Team. After graduating from Hancock College, Phillip then went on to San Diego State.

Paul was born in 1978. In his teens he worked as a cart boy at the Santa Maria Country Club. When Mike Valdez first came to SMCC as a cart boy, Paul helped train him! Paul ended up being a Professional Race Car Driver, sponsored by *Red Bull* and *General Motors.*

Ron and Marcia have always loved sports and participated in their sons' activities. Ron was President of South Side Little League one year.

With the busy lives they have always led, it is not surprising that they didn't join the Santa Maria Country Club until 1991.

Ron served on the SMCC Board of Directors for three years as Tournament Chairman. Marcia has served as President of the Women's Division, first in 2008-2009, then again in 2015-2016. What an asset these two have been to the club.

ROBERT "RANDE" AND LINDA DOWNER

"From a bramble bush I picked a rose."

"Sorry girls he's taken."

Rande Downer didn't join the Santa Maria Country Club until 1990, but what an asset he has been since he joined. He served on the Board of Directors in various capacities: Vice-President; Secretary; Membership and Bylaws Committee Chair; and Certified Handicap Chair.

Rande was born on May 13, 1946 to Charles Robert "Bob" (master barber and shop owner) and Darlene Lucille (Bricken) Downer in Flint, Michigan. He lived in Flint until the age of 16 when the family moved to Sacramento, California.

Whether it has been pursuing higher education, military service, professional career, professional organizations, etc. he has approached each and every endeavor with a rare zeal for every goal to be attained.

He served his country with the U. S. Air Force as a SSgt (honorable discharge), and is a Vietnam Veteran. Then he not only got his Bachelor of Science degree in Business Administration, Organizational Management, with honors, from CSU Sacramento (1977), he went on to get his Master of Science, School Business Administration degree from Pepperdine University, with honors (1980).

Rande's professional career is just as impressive as his education. He was Director of Transportation for Hemet Unified School District, and Kern County Office of Education. He was Chief of Business and Operations, Hanford High School, Santa Maria High School, and Orcutt school district.

After his professional career, he formed his own consulting firm, Carousel Consulting, Inc. He also was a graduate school professor.

Linda has been a very active participant in various activities at SMCC since 1990. She was a low handicap golfer in the Women's Division. Her hobbies include walking, reading and working with her "posies." When I asked Rande if he helped her with the flowers, he laughed and said, "I mostly get to clean and vacuum the dirt out of the car when she brings them home."

Rande is father of sons Craig Downer, Bend, Oregon, Clayton Downer (deceased), daughter Stacy, and granddaughter Shelby.

One of his great joys in retirement is photography. One of his best photographs graces the cover of this book. It is entitled *Lone Golfer.*

KAYE AND DOTTIE LYONS

———•◆•———

Kaye and Dottie Lyons were married in Bakersfield, California, in 1994, and moved to Santa Maria to begin their new life together. They had both been successful business persons in their previous lives, and they both had a passion for golf. They were each other's great mature love.

They joined the Santa Maria Country Club in 1994 and both became heavily involved in its activities. In addition to mixed couple's golf, Kaye joined the Portuguese Golf Association (PGA) which was a group of men organized at SMCC to have fun and play golf. They chose someone to act as President each year, had a scheduled tee time each Thursday, and all enjoyed great golf games together. There was a strong bond among them and many lifetime friendships were formed. When they could no longer play the game of golf, many of them would meet for breakfast on Saturday mornings to share stories together and get "updated" on what was happening at the club. Kaye served as President from 2009 until his death August 13, 2014.

Dottie had already been heavily involved, in her previous life, in many organizations throughout Santa Maria. But golf, and the Santa Maria Country Club, has been at the centerpiece of her life since she fell in love with Kaye. She was President of the Women's Board, 1999-2000. She is the Sunshine Chair on the SMCC Board, who takes pictures at various functions, delivers food or flowers (e.g. illness or bereavement).

Kaye and Dottie were blessed with 20 years of marriage and his death left a big hole in her heart.

KEITH AND GLENDA NATZKE

———— •◆• ————

Keith was born December 26, 1933 in Ashippun, Wisconsin. The family moved to Denver, Colorado when Keith was eight years old. He attended North High School in Denver, graduating in 1951. He was employed with Martin-Marietta, and while there he was acquainted with another Martin-Marietta employee named Mike Gaughen. Ironically, they both ended up their careers at Vandenberg Air Force Base, now live in Santa Maria, both joined the Santa Maria Country Club and love golf.

Glenda Ramsey was born February 19, 1936 in Elk City, Oklahoma. This was when the entire country was still struggling to survive the Great Depression. Glenda's grandfather, Sturgeon Alfred Cox, who had owned quite a lot of land in Oklahoma, lost it all. He packed up and moved to Santa Maria, California. Glenda had two brothers (she was the "middle" child) and when she was six years old, the entire family moved to Santa Maria to live with grandpa. He fixed up a little house for them to live in.

Grandpa Cox was quite a guy and was a beloved man. He owned a gas station in Santa Maria during the worst economic times. People would need gas for their cars but didn't have the money and he would pump them some gas for them to "get by." After he died October 4, 1951 they named a street after him. Glenda was attending Santa Maria High School at the time. She graduated in 1954.

When Glenda was about 7 or 8 years old, she and her brother rode their bikes down toward Waller Park where they would go to fish in the pond. As they were riding by the entrance to the Santa Maria Country Club, like most little kids they were curious about the place. A couple of golfers saw them and asked them if they would like to "caddie" for them. The kids asked what a caddie did. The golfers said "We'll show you how." After they were finished, the golfers paid them each a dollar! Wow! Glenda never dreamed that one day she would someday be playing golf on that beautiful course.

Years later, Glenda worked at Vandenberg where she met the love of her life — Keith Natzke. They got married on August 16, 1987. It was ten years before they joined the Santa Maria Country Club. They immediately became very active in golf and the social activities of the club. Keith served as President of the Board of Directors from 2011-2014. What a blessing it is to have this couple as members.

LORIN AND JEAN HUBBARD

———•◆•———

Lorin Hubbard was born October 13, 1924 in Lewistown, Montana. In 1942, he enlisted in the U. S. Navy. World War II was underway and many skills were needed. He wound up being stationed at the Naval Air Station in Alameda, California. The extensive training he received at their Aircraft Mechanic School paved the way for a lifetime of employment with major airlines all over the world.

Gloria Jean Gibbs was born July 27, 1927 in Martinez, California where she attended elementary school in a two room school house. Her family moved to the Concord area where she attended and graduated from Mt. Diablo Union High School in 1945. After high school she worked at a couple of different jobs before she received a job with Southwest Airlines.

Jean and Lorin Hubbard got married on August 30, 1952 in Reno, Nevada. They were over there having a good time with friends and couldn't figure out who was going to be the maid of honor, the best man, etc., so the Justice of the Peace finally said, "All of you get up here so we can get on with the ceremony!" They spent their honeymoon going fishing with friends. Sixty-four years later this cute couple still feels like they hit the jackpot. And, NO, they don't have a wedding picture!

During Lorin's 35 years with PANAM, then with Boeing, the Hubbards lived and worked all over the globe — Guam, Hong Kong, Istanbul, Bangkok, Kuwait, Brazil (Rio de Janeiro). Lorin and Jean made many lifelong friends during those many years of working abroad. They remain close friends with one couple from Australia today.

On Guam, on November 11, 1962, they survived the killer typhoon, *Karen,* but the house in which they were living was destroyed. They pulled a heavy table as far away from the louvered windows as possible and got up on it. The roof was completely blown off and all the windows were blown out, but they came through the storm unharmed. Winds reached a velocity of 205 miles per hour.

The horrible event that changed Lorin and Jean's lives forever happened when the madman Saddam Hussein gave the order for Iraq to invade Kuwait and seize hostages.

Lorin and Jean had lived in Kuwait for five years when it was invaded. They (and many others) were taken and held as hostages. They were taken away from their living quarters by bus with very few minutes to pack what belongings they could carry. WATER was a must as the heat in the desert was over 100 degrees. One lady had failed to pack much water so Jean offered to share hers. The lady asked, "Is it cold?" Lorin said, "No, lady. The ice machine is broken."

Lorin (back row, left) with the male hostages.

The first hostages Saddam agreed to release were the women and children. At first Jean insisted that she would not go without her husband; Lorin finally persuaded her that she should go on and do what she could to get their affairs back home (Seattle) in order. Jean was put on a plane and went back to Seattle via many plane changes, where Boeing (Lorin's employer) provided her with a condo and paid all her bills while she began her long wait, praying for Lorin's safe return. Finally, all of the male hostages were put on a plane to Frankfurt where they could catch flights to their homeland. Gaunt and raggedy, Lorin finally arrived in Seattle where Jean had waited for more than three months.

Lorin and Jean moved to Santa Maria and joined the Santa Maria Country Club on 9/11/2001! Words cannot express the joy they find in retiring in this wonderful place called Santa Maria. They have enjoyed the golf, the comradery, and all the friendships formed at SMCC. Lorin and Jean have played golf in many places and many countries, but there is no place like home — Santa Maria!

Lorin and Jean would like to thank Pat Chandler, a neighbor, a friend and a member of the Santa Maria Country Club for her friendship, and her many acts of kindness over these past fifteen years. What a wonderful lady!

PART 3

CLUB STAFF MEMBERS

SANTA MARIA COUNTRY CLUB STAFF

———•◆•———

Everything prior to this chapter is about the people, the circumstances, and the events that created and sustained this wonderful place called the Santa Maria Country Club. Now it is time to introduce you to the people who not only brighten our lives, but keep this place running smoothly.

Joe Priddy, General Manager

Joe and his lovely wife, Linda, came to us in 2010. They were born and grew up in the great state of Texas. They have four children — one girl and three boys — who have all embarked on their own careers.

Joe has an incredible background, not just in golf but management in general. He has the firm foundation which equips him to manage this diverse club, which includes tennis, swimming and social events. He has had to make some "tough calls" since coming to SMCC, but his wisdom and experience have served him well.

TRACY BOWLES, HEAD GOLF PRO

A lifetime lover of golf and a Golf Professional since 1982, Tracy has enjoyed teaching, working and playing at Santa Maria Country Club since 1995. SMCC hired him two years after a major accident left him with two broken legs and two broken arms. His determination to get back to the game he loves kept him focused. He says the best professional and personal years of his life have been spent at the Santa Maria Country Club.

"I always enjoy coming to work at SMCC. The members are my second family, as we have had great relationships and wonderful times together" says Tracy. Even in times of great physical pain, he never gives up. When I feel like whining or giving up, I think of Tracy and kick myself!

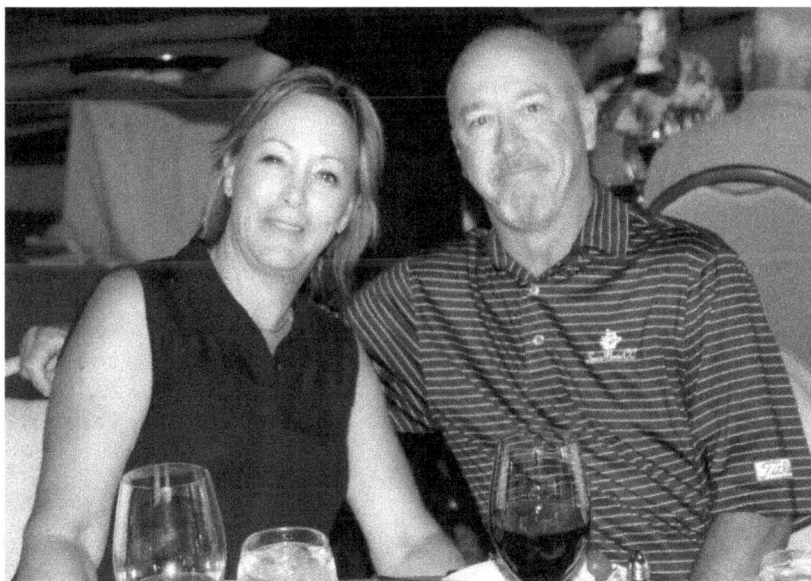

"Mary, light of my life."

MIKE VALDEZ, HEAD GOLF PRO (2009-2016)

Mike Valdez, Head Golf Pro with Santa Maria Country Club since 2009.

Mike was born and raised on the Central Coast and was introduced to golf while attending Allan Hancock College. A calendar year after his first round of golf (101), Mike played his way into the AHC Golf Team. Mike started his employment at SMCC in April 1993 as a "cart boy." Six months later, he found himself as a full-time student and junior college athlete, while still working part- time to fund his education. In 1996, Mike was given an opportunity to work toward achieving his PGA Professional Classification, and in 2004 he achieved that goal. In 2009, Mike reached another of his goals, becoming Head Golf Professional at SMCC, which he considers his second family.

Mike and and his lovely wife, Dianna, and their three children: Nevaeh 5-1/2 (heaven spelled backwards), Rowan, 4, and Camden, 2. Another child is "on the way" so then he will have a golf foursome!

STEVE CUTTS
PGA ASSISTANT GOLF PRO
2009 — PRESENT

Steve was born in Los Angeles, CA in 1949. He graduated from Culver City High School in 1967. He was a 3-sport letterman each year (football, basketball, baseball), and was nominated to the Athletic Hall of Fame. He then attended Cal Poly SLO on a baseball scholarship, and obtained his degree in Physical Education.

Steve then played one year for an independent league (Class A) affiliate of the California Angels. He then taught/coached five years of high school, earning two CIF baseball titles and five league championships.

In 2001, he earned his PGA membership. He also married his beautiful wife, Sandy, on September 10, 2001. Busy year, Steve!

Steve and Sandy on their wedding day in 2001.

Julia at work in the Pro Shop.

Julia and husband, Andrew, with daughter, Marlowe.

Julia is a life-long resident of the Central Coast. Born and raised in Lompoc, Julia began playing golf with her twin sister, Justine, with the support of their parents, Jerry and Susan.

Julia competed for the Lompoc High School Girls Golf Team, earning the League MVP title all four years. She continued competing while on the Cal Poly SLO team, and it was around this time that her passion for teaching the game grew when she began coaching with *The first Tee Central Coast.*

Santa Maria Country Club Pro Shop, circa. 1960s. Pictured are the SMCC Golf Pro, Frank Hocknell, left, and Carroll Sharp, right.

Photo courtesy of John Eggert.

130

In between marrying her husband, Andrew, and her graduation from Cal Poly with a Bachelor's Degree in History, Julia continued to expand her coaching with *The First Tee*. She began heading a new site at the Santa Maria Country Club, which eventually led to her joining the SMCC team in the pro shop.

As of 2016, Julia and her husband, Andrew, have welcomed their daughter, Marlowe, into the world. Julie is continuing to grow the game of golf with juniors on the Central Coast through *The First Tee,* coaching the SLO High School Girls Golf Team, and multiple junior programs through the Santa Maria Country Club.

JOSE PENA
GOLF CART SUPERVISOR

Jose was born in El Salvador and moved to Santa Maria in 1984. He attended Allan Hancock College and played soccer there for two years.

Santa Maria Country Club hired Jose in 1994, and he has been with us ever since. His smiling face is like a ray of sunshine to all the SMCC members. He enjoys working with SMCC members and it shows!

Jose and his wife Debbie live in Orcutt where they have raised their two children. His hobbies are refereeing youth soccer games and swimming.

OFFICE STAFF AND OTHERS

Pictured below are the Office Staff who are the heartbeat of the Santa Maria Country Club. They are the first people that the public meets when they walk in the front door.

L to R: Linda Johnson, Melissa Rugge, Casandra Carnino, Bert Mayor.
Not available for picture: Amy Murguia (on maternity leave).

LINDA JOHNSON

Linda has been with SMCC since 2001. She is a native Santa Marian and started out as a food and beverage server. Her current role is Hostess, but she is performing the role of Events Director/Member Relations in the absence of Amy Murguia.

MELISSA RUGGE

Melissa was born and raised in Bryn Mawr, PA and attended Berklee College of Music in Boston. She and her husband now live in Santa Ynez. She also has an accounting background and is the one responsible for keeping our records straight!

CASSANDRA CARNINO

Cassandra is the newest member of the office staff. She is the friendly face who greets you when you enter the office. She was born and raised in Santa Maria and she assists the other staff members.

BERT MAYOR

Bert was born and raised in a small town in New Jersey. She moved to Santa Maria in 1966, mostly for the weather – NO SNOW! She has worked in the Administrative Office at the Santa Maria Country Club since 1995, and enjoys the challenges and diversity the job has given her. She is the person who mentioned to me that a book had never been written on the history of the Santa Maria Country Club. In her 21 years at SMCC she has experienced a lot. She enjoys the friendship of members and co-workers.

SWIMMING POOL
SANTA MARIA COUNTRY CLUB

Photo courtesy of John Eggert

Santa Maria Country Club swimming pool, ca. 1960s.

It wasn't until sometime after fire gutted the second clubhouse in 1954 and a rebuild took place that a swimming pool was added to the Santa Maria Country Club facilities. Above is a photo of that first pool, where Scott Bronnel was the instructor.

When the new modern clubhouse and its facilities were built in 1999, the new pool was constructed near the tennis courts. Although it is a regulation size pool, no lane lines were installed so it doesn't qualify to be utilized for competitive swim meets.

Here's the biography of the man who has been the swim coach and pool manager since the inception of the new pool in 2000.

Santa Maria Country Club swimming pool, 2016.

SERAFIN VILLARETE

On June 2, 1946, Serafin Villarete was born, the fifth son of six children born to his parents, Magdalena and Tomas. Life was very simple in Panganiban, Philippines. Their small house was next to the river where Serafin spent hours fishing and swimming. When he was nine years of age, his older brother, Ulpiano, brought him to Manilla to live with him. Even in elementary school, Serafin was an excellent swimmer who worked hard and won meets.

At Jose Rizal High School he received a full scholarship as a swimmer. The records he set in high school in the 100 and 200 breaststroke competition are still standing.

Recruited by the National University of the Philippines, he swam for one year. During that time he represented his university at the World University Games in Tokyo, Japan.

In 1967, American coach Don Gambril, who was the American Olympic coach and also coach of Long Beach State College, came to the Philippines to conduct clinics for the Philippine swimmers. He recruited seven Filipino swimmers to come to the United States and train for the Olympics in Mexico City. Serafin was one of two swimmers academically qualified to swim for Long Beach State College. He represented his college in the California Collegiate Athletic Association swimming championship in 1968 where he placed second in the 100 yard and in the 200. Unfortunately, having trained for the CCAA, he missed qualifying for the Mexico Olympics by hundredths of a second.

By this time Serafin had met Janet Decker and they were married on May 25, 1968. Since Serafin had ordered a "relay team," they proceeded to have four sons, all of which were good swimmers.

Serafin at "his" pool.

Serafin and Janet Villarete.

In 2000, Serafin and Janet moved to Santa Maria to be nearer their two grandsons. Serafin was able to work at the Santa Maria Country Club as the pool manager, and also coach for Santa Maria Swim Club. Later he also coached for St. Joseph High School, and then at Righetti High School.

Now in his 70s, Serafin enjoys taking care of "his" pool at SMCC, life guarding, and teaching students to swim.

Janet and Serafin with their "relay team, "which consists of their four sons.
L to R: David, Andrew, Janet, Christopher, Serafin, and Brian.

CLOSING REMARKS

This is so much more than a "history" book. It also gives you a brief glimpse into the lives of just a few of the current members, who willingly shared their stories about their years at the Santa Maria Country Club.

This wonderful club has been an integral part of our community for the past 95 years. As you will read in the first part of this book, it came into being on November 16, 1921. People with vision and influence set the stage for its beginning, but it was the working class that made it a reality. We must never forget that.

Right here within the city limits of Santa Maria we have it all — a beautiful 18-hole golf course, tennis courts, regulation size swimming pool, beautiful clubhouse with large dining room and full-service bar overlooking the 18th fairway, pro shop stocked with apparel, golf equipment, etc.

But by far the most important asset the club has is the friendly welcoming people. From the minute you walk in the front door to the time you exit, you are treated as an old friend. All members and employees have a stake in its success.

Come grow with us as we journey into our 96th year!

Ollie M. Kirby, Author

NAME INDEX

———— ◆ ————

The Arrow Camera Team
From L to R: Kayla Sauer, Margrit Holmes, Marissa Flores and James Manville

Meet the wonderful team who
turned our book into a treasure!